IN BROKEN IMAGES

Feminist Tales for a
Different Teacher Education

IN BROKEN IMAGES

Feminist Tales for a Different Teacher Education

Erica McWilliam

Foreword by Patti Lather

Teachers College, Columbia University
New York and London

The poem "In Broken Images" is reprinted from COLLECTED POEMS 1975 by Robert Graves. Copyright © 1975 by Robert Graves. Reprinted by permission of Oxford University Press, Inc., and A. P. Watt Ltd. on behalf of The Trustees of the Robert Graves Copyright Trust.

Published by Teachers College Press, 1234 Amsterdam Avenue, New York, NY 10027

Library of Congress Cataloging-in-Publication Data

McWilliam, Erica.
    In broken images : feminist tales for a different teacher education / Erica McWilliam ; foreword by Patti Lather.
      p. cm.
    Includes bibliographical references (p.) and index.
    ISBN 0–8077–3387–3 (alk. paper).—ISBN 0–8077–3386–5 (pbk. : alk. paper)
      1. Teachers—Training of. 2. Teachers—Training of—Research.
    3. Feminism and education.   I. Title.
    LB1707M38   1995
    370.71—dc20   94–31503

ISBN 0–8077–3386–5 (paper)
ISBN 0–8077–3387–3 (cloth)

Printed on acid-free paper
Manufactured in the United States of America

02 01 00 99 98 97 96 95   8 7 6 5 4 3 2 1

To Hazel Cryle, my mother,
one of the great teachers.

IN BROKEN IMAGES

He is quick, thinking in clear images;
I am slow, thinking in broken images.

He becomes dull, trusting to his clear images;
I become sharp, mistrusting my broken images.

Trusting his images, he assumes their relevance;
Mistrusting my images, I question their relevance.

Assuming their relevance, he assumes the fact;
Questioning their relevance, I question the fact.

When the fact fails him, he questions his senses;
When the fact fails me, I approve my senses.

He continues quick and dull in his clear images;
I continue slow and sharp in my broken images.

He in a new confusion of his understanding;
I in a new understanding of my confusion.

Robert Graves

CONTENTS

FOREWORD

This book is based on a doctoral thesis from Australia for which I served as outside examiner in 1992. In this foreword, I delineate the theoretical terrain of the book in order to address its usefulness for contesting and re-orienting both teacher education and research methodology.

The Teacher Education Project

In terms of the history of professionalization in teaching, David Larabee (1992) traces the contest for authority in colleges of education between university-based administrative studies, teacher education with its roots in normal schools, and educational psychology with its history as the originary site for the scientific study of teaching and learning. Larabee's central argument is that the present moment is witness to the ascendancy of teacher education within colleges of education, a rise warranted by claims to research-based evidence on effective teaching techniques and command of the rhetorical ground of school improvement. Tracking the interactions of power and knowledge in the shaping of colleges of education, Larabee lists the newly dominant language of teacher education: career professionals, clinical faculty, professional development of schools, lead teachers. No happy story or "comfortable scenario" (p. 126), Larabee's arguments mark the teacher professionalization movement as "contested terrain," as he calls for critique that works "to criticize and question, to vex with precision" (pp. 142–143).

Such is the project of this book. Tracking the movements of discursive reformulation in educational thought, McWilliam draws on postmodernism, feminism, discourse studies, and critical theorizing to challenge both traditional foundations of knowledge in teacher education and more avant-garde critical reformulations. According to McWilliam, teacher education is characterized by a weak and ambiguous knowledge base and a human engineering model fed by a positivist research climate where critical/political teacher education by no means occupies some innocent space outside of a master narrative. Advocating, instead, a within/against critique, she hopes to "revitalize" the impoverished debate about the nature of teacher socialization. In terms of the dominant discourses of teacher education, she notes how a paternal discourse of managerial efficiency and practicality has wed a maternal discourse of therapy, resulting in a depoliticization of teaching via a romantic discourse of individual differences and self-esteem. Wanting to educate teachers for postmodern times, her central argument is the importance of helping students understand the power relations in which teachers work without being defeated by them.

In her "neo-feminist tale" of leaving behind the "quick and dull" oppositions that structure representations of how teacher competence is acquired, McWilliam engages with the following theoretical and methodological questions: What does it mean to "stand at an angle" in refusing to work out of the old certainties of "oppositional/critical," technocratic/bureaucratic, or psychologized/humanistic vocabularies of teacher preparation? How can the theoretical labor of feminisms of difference be brought to the arena of teacher education policy and curriculum? Methodologically, what does it mean to work toward "more telling tales"?

Positioning teacher education policy as a struggle over language, McWilliam notes the complexity of studying language as framed within broader networks of discursive practices—disciplinary, institutional, and societal. In order to provide tools for negotiating competing ways of talking about teaching and learning, she draws on the resources of contemporary social theory to better navigate the contested political nature of educational work. Engaging with students to develop a language of critique that is about the capacity to think within and through various theoretical perspectives, the goal is to become uncomfortable in dominant discursive orders. Additionally, to recognize the discursive structures within which contemporary debates in education are embedded (e.g., theory-practice, asymmetries of power, and the production of knowledge within discursive formations and social-historical conditions) is to move both within and against already sedimented critical sociologies of the education/economy interface, such as the "predictability of neo-marxist conspiracy theories" and "them versus us" category schemas.

It is here that feminisms of difference are called on to create a space in which a different practice becomes possible via experimenting with our own meanings, practices, and confoundings. Here, speaking from shifting subject positions and occupying zones of legitimacy only to dismantle them or exploit them as sites of intervention, McWilliam works within/against the dominant, contesting its borders, tracing complicity, moving into some place I am presently calling feminist efforts toward a doubled science, both science and not-science. To position one's work as both within the disciplinary discourse of the human sciences and as a wanderer outside of the science in which it purports to be is to capture the vitality of the deviations that elude taxonomies. The concept of a doubled science, then, gestures toward a proliferation of eccentric kinds of science, "as much nomadology as sociology" (Brantlinger & Ulin, 1993, p. 35), in addressing the question of practices of science within the context of post-foundational discourse theory.

Hence, located within the long-term reorientation of inquiry in many fields of study, particularly the social sciences and professional studies, her work is well outside the binary logic of qualitative/quantitative. Using her empirical work to explore a methodology of interactive interviews, participants analyze and explain their own writing and engage as co-theorists toward reciprocally educative processes. Such research practices move toward telling a new tale of teacher preservice socialization, enacting "risky experimentation across and even beyond," within and against praxis-oriented research. Arguing that you cannot do it differently and say it the same in "the comfort zone of a familiar language system," she pushes on to productive outcomes— telling moments that effect a difference that makes a difference where "more telling" means addressing multiple versus binary category schemes and mobilizing reflexivity about the "expert" positioning of critical intellectuals who are taken to task for their refusal to provide concrete suggestions.

The "linguistic turn" moved against humanism and the privileging of consciousness. The "reflexive turn" in the social sciences undercut the reign of rational abstraction and the flight into objectivity. The "postmodern turn" makes the doubled move of both endorsing Lyotardian "small narratives" against metanarratives AND de-naturalizes narrative conventions via "double-coded narratives" which "structurally both install and subvert the teleology, closure, and causality of narrative" (Hutcheon, 1989, p. 63). Each captures movements around language and posthumanism and the loss of foundations (Spanos, 1993). Within such a landscape, McWilliam is well enough equipped methodologically to be able to render an account that gestures toward complexity without getting lost in the telling. Using textual forms of data display in ways that progressively complicate one's intellectual givens, she locates her work outside a victory narrative, as a doubled practice that both categorizes and then displaces that categorization. This is about foregrounding the limits, the necessary misfirings of representational efforts, where inquiry becomes a laboratory for discovering the rules by which truths are produced.

I do have some reservations that the lines between Althusser and Derrida are not as clear as she draws. Althusser can as much be called the first poststructuralist and the last structuralist in his gesturing toward the roles of the unconscious and language and the limits of the dialectic. And Derrida's deferral of a confrontation with Marxism is more about strategy within the context of French intellectual history than about the political limits of deconstruction. In a 1993 interview, Derrida states,

> I always abstained from criticizing Marxism head-on. . . . What I sought to say would have been amalgamated and massively translated too quickly into a problematic that dissatisfied me. . . . However, I meant to read Marx my way when the time came . . . in order to jump a few steps, today, when in France any reference to Marx has become forbidden, impossible, immediately catalogued, I have a real desire to speak about Marx, to teach Marx . . . the manner in which the discourse I find myself engaged in . . . signifies for someone who knows how to read it that Marx is always there (pp. 192, 201, 218).

Additionally, I am less sanguine about the line she traces from the usefulness of Foucault for feminism versus her suspiciousness of Derridean "play" and Nietzschean "gay science." At work here is some refusal of the Nietzschean moment in social theory, some refusal of the anti-Hegelianism, the anti-dialectic, the anti-phenomenology of the subject that undergirds such contemporary philosophers as Deleuze and Derrida. Foucault, too, of course, figures in all of this, although he is more easily recuperable into the liberal humanism within which we are so deeply inscribed, even though Foucault insisted on underwriting his project with Nietzsche (Mahon, 1992).

Anti-foundationalism is as much a de-centering of philosophy to social criticism as it is anything else. This doesn't mean social criticism isn't grounded in something. But that something can no longer be assumed to be philosophy, particularly abstract, universalized philosophy (Greene, 1994). It is not that (local) efforts to transform and commitments to social justice don't continue; it is that they proceed without either universally legitimating metanarratives or pretentions of the intellectual as the great transformer, the master of truth and justice. McWilliam has crafted her grounding in empirical work that blurs the genre between research and pedagogy in the midst of the "galloping theory" where we try to stay ahead of perpetually re-forming problematics (McWilliam, 1993). Bringing these shifts in thought to the doing of inquiry is a project that underscores the impor-tance of refusing an anti-science position. Whatever "neo-feminism," postpositivism and poststructural feminism might mean, work like this helps create another imaginary for feminist research in education.

—Patti Lather

References

Brantlinger, P., & Ulin, D. (1993). Policing nomads. *Cultural Critique, 25,* 33–64.

Derrida, J. (1993). Politics and friendship: An interview with Jacques Derrida. In E. A. Kaplan & M. Sprinker (Eds.), *The Althusserean legacy* (pp. 183–231). London: Verso.

Greene, M. (1994). Epistemology and educational research: The influence of recent approaches to knowledge. In L. Darling-Hammond (Ed.), *Review of Research in Education,* Vol. 20. Washington, DC: The American Educational Research Association.

Hutcheon, L. (1989). *The politics of postmodernism.* New York: Routledge.

Larabee, D. (1992). Power, knowledge, and the rationalization of teaching: A genealogy of the movement to professionalize teaching. *Harvard Educa-tional Review, 62*(2), 123–154.

Mahon, M. (1992). *Foucault's Nietzschean genealogy: Truth, power, and the subject.* Albany: State University of New York.

McWilliam, E. (1993). Post haste: Plodding research and galloping theory. *Brit-ish Journal of Sociology of Education, 14*(1), 199–205.

Spanos, W. (1993). *The end of education: Toward posthumanism.* Minneapolis: Uni-versity of Minnesota Press.

ACKNOWLEDGMENTS

I am pleased to be able to acknowledge the people who have given me support and encouragement in completing this book. I would particularly want to thank my doctoral supervisor, John Knight (University of Queensland), for his unflagging enthusiasm for my research; my editors at Teachers College Press, Brian Ellerbeck, Melissa Mashburn, and Karl Nyberg; and Wendy Morgan (Queensland University of Technology), all of whom gave valuable assistance with the manuscript. My thanks also to my colleagues at QUT, Noeline Kyle, Peter O'Brien, Jacqueline Hamilton-Lavery, Gordon Tait, Daphne Meadmore, Jill Brannock, Brian Hoepper, and Peter Taylor, without whose professional and personal support the task would have been much more difficult. Other academic colleagues—Leo Bartlett (University of Central Queensland); Bob Lingard, Fazal Rizvi, Paige Porter, and Greer Johnson (University of Queensland); David Kirk (Deakin University); Patti Lather (Ohio State University); and Jenny Gore and Jim Ladwig (University of Newcastle)—have also been most supportive. My thanks to Richard Smith and Ted D'Urso for their belief in the quality of my work at Masters level. To Mark Cryle and Barbara Sullivan-Windle I express thanks for their help with sources, and to Peter Cryle (French Department, University of Queensland) and Sandra Scott for their unflagging faith in the project.

INTRODUCTION

This book documents my attempt to teach myself about initial teacher education as a critical feminist project. I have co-opted the title of Robert Graves's poem "In Broken Images" because I want to signal that the sort of writing I have done here breaks from the conventions of traditional teacher education texts. It *re*presents teacher education as a fragmented, not a unified, project. While Robert Graves was a classicist who knew nothing of current debates in social theory, his metaphors are useful for a feminist writing out of new vocabularies and standing at an angle to mainstream educational writing. In identifying with the oppositional stance of the poet, I am refusing to work out of old certainties, whether these are epistemological, methodological, or stylistic. The task is ambitious because I want to challenge the culture of initial teacher education by examining the way particular textual practices shape, and thereby limit, the way teacher educators understand their work.

Each of the chapters that follow takes the form of an essay that attempts to indicate how recent developments in feminist social theory can be usefully applied to an aspect of the work of teacher educators. I indicate how contemporary feminisms have assisted me as a teacher educator and researcher to make strategic interventions across a range of educational endeavors, from policy analysis to pedagogy, from research to the "reality" of field experiences. The logic of the sequence of chapters is not linear, although connections are made between one essay and the next. Each essay is multi-tiered, raising issues of theory and methodology in order to apply these to specific concerns in teacher education. Therefore, readers do not have to start at the beginning, but may use their own interests as a guide.

I am unapologetic about the pervasiveness of theorizing in the text, although I acknowledge that I am writing out of vocabularies that may be unfamiliar to some readers. I believe that it is not possible to make much-needed reforms in teacher education without changing the way we talk about it.

Chapter 1, *In Clear Images: Political Agendas for Teacher Education Policy,* maps a discursive terrain of teacher education policy. It examines the reform agendas of policy makers and the reforming agendas of those who critique educational policy documents. As an introduction to this analysis, I describe some of the concerns contemporary feminist writers have about critical scholarship in general. Among these concerns is the predictable nature of debates between academics and those who also have a stake in designing and maintaining teacher education courses. I try to demonstrate that poststructural theory can help to move critiques on from the predictability of neo-Marxist conspiracy theories through attending to the way words are contested and colonized in policy documents and related educational texts.

In Chapter 2, *In Broken Images: Feminisms of Difference for Teacher Education Research,* I elaborate on the way new feminist theorizing challenges "modernist" traditions of educational research. Given that much current feminist scholarship draws on New French Theory, I demonstrate a link between the ideas of three French writers—Louis Althusser, Jacques Derrida, and Michel Foucault—and feminist educational writing. I show how feminist theory challenges the idea that research ought to be separate from pedagogy, before moving on to critique mainstream traditions of teacher education research methodology.

My rationale for Chapter 3, *Quick and Dull: The Folkloric Discourses of Teacher Education,* is the need for better scholarship about teacher education. I argue that, in Foucault's terms, a "regime of truth" has been established that draws its legitimacy from a number of "definitive" studies. I note the binary logic through which teacher socialization texts have been constructed. While the role of critical pedagogues in challenging the effects of this has been important, that role has been limited not simply by its own marginal position in teacher education literature but by its reliance on "them and us" readings of teacher education practices. Using feminist methodology, I deconstruct one such critique in order to illustrate a different reading of teacher education culture.

Chapters 4 and 5 are a record of research conducted with pre-service teachers using new feminist theory. In documenting my work as a teacher/researcher, they present a case study in the use of the theoretical terrain outlined in earlier essays. Chapter 4, *Slow and Sharp: Reconstructing Pre-service Teacher Socialization,* describes the professional socialization of a group of undergraduate students in ways different from the idealism-to-realism story that has become a truism of teacher education literature. In Chapter 5, *Questioning the Fact: Advocacy in Initial Teacher Education Research,* my research tale becomes part of a pedagogic process involving the research participants. Both chapters display the written and oral texts of students through the lens that I constructed as a feminist researcher. For those who are interested in what they might actually *do* with students, as well as with texts, when working out of feminisms of difference, these chapters may provide some useful insights. However, they are not intended as blueprints for action.

Finally, Chapter 6, Post*Script:* Re-*presenting Broken Images,* is a reflection on the processes and outcomes of my research-as-pedagogy. It provides a postscript about the professional futures of the research participants as well as some reflections on what I learned as a teacher educator from working "inside-out" in my research. I attempt to summarize the challenges of providing a postmodern teacher education project and the impossibility of doing this while working out of old teacher education plots.

In Broken Images

Feminist Tales for a
Different Teacher Education

CHAPTER 1

In Clear Images
Political Agendas for Teacher Education Policy

NEW FEMINISM AND EDUCATIONAL CRITIQUE

This introduces what is essentially a feminist tale about teacher education policy and its analysis. It is "political" in three respects. First, it is about educational practices, which 20 years of critical educational writing have demonstrated to be always value-laden, never neutral. It is political too in that, while it is unashamedly feminist, it makes problematic how this term might be understood in a postmodern context. Most importantly, it is a tale about power—the power to define teacher education policy—not only in the sense of repression and prohibition but also as incitement to discourse and the production of knowledge (Eco, 1986, p. 242).

My construction of this story about teacher education policy (and those stories that follow) differs in certain fundamental ways from more conventional texts I have read in my own professional work as a pre-service teacher, a practicing teacher, and a teacher educator. This is because it is at one and the same time a theorizing of and a strategy for reconstructive debate around teacher education practices. It is also because it is important to me as a teacher that others have access to very useful ways of *applying* feminist ideas and frameworks to perennial problems in the teacher education project. Unfortunately, discipline-specific and at times rarefied vocabularies can and do limit the size of a potential audience. Maxine Greene (1993) quite rightly makes the point that readership may well have been overestimated by critical educational writers in the past, while the present deconstructive trend may only exacerbate the problem of "a relatively small and precious world" of informed readers (p. 208). So while current feminist writers may speak quite accurately of "well-rehearsed" arguments in theorizing modernism, postmodernism, and education (Roman, 1993,

p. 20), it must be remembered that, for large numbers of people committed to good educational practice, these ideas have not appeared
in any meaningful script, let alone reached a moment of rehearsal.
My motivation for saying this should not be mistaken for anti-
intellectualism. As I have argued elsewhere (McWilliam, 1993a, p. 3),
quite the reverse is in fact true. My concern is that so much of the
theoretical labor of contemporary feminism ought to inform more sub-
stantially the general debates about worthwhile teacher education that
are currently taking place.

In calling this a tale, I am writing in a relatively new tradition of
scholarship born out of the crises of self-definition that feminists have
had in examining the legitimacy of knowledge claims. As a reader and
writer of social theory, I engage with educational ideas during a time
when there is no ideological safety, no pure position, no vantage point
beyond the site of knowledge production. This can, of course, bring its
own sort of paralysis—what I have termed Post Modernist Tension
(PMT) (McWilliam, 1993a). PMT has encouraged a rush to play the
often cynical game of "first past the post." The result has at times been
a scholarship that is sustained more by narcissism than by need. When
fashionable theory lapses into cynicism, the moral high ground can
easily be occupied by those for whom quietism is a virtue, while writing against oppression is relegated to the ranks of the Neanderthal. It
is for this reason that so many contemporary feminists have refused
the prefix *post*. Yet it is also post literature (poststructuralism, postmodernism) that has generated so many corrective moments for critical
scholarship. And it is for this reason that many feminists adopt
counter-strategies that put skepticism to work rather than surety (e.g.,
Ellsworth, 1989; Gore, 1993; Lather, 1991a, 1991b).

Contemporary feminist poststructuralist texts are therefore more
likely to struggle against their own tendency to grand and romantic
narrative about all-encompassing oppositions between oppressors and
oppressed. They are less likely to urge sudden and radical transforma-
tions of student teachers by means of a formula for empowerment of
future teachers as critically reflective practitioners. The danger here of
course is that it becomes almost too easy to substitute immobility for
radical critique. If every system is dangerous, a cynic might well ask,
why struggle to replace one with another?

In keeping with the postmodern appeal to the local and precarious rather than the global and the certain, I acknowledge the problem
of past and present "macro" analyses of teacher education in general-
izing about the way notions like relevance are constructed across institutional sites. Yet I am heartened by the fact that neo-feminist writers

do not see a rejection of holism and meta-narrative as a retreat from grappling with "big" issues such as poverty/classism, racism, sexism, and other forms of social injustice. It is important, however, to make problematic the very clarity with which such stories have been told, including our own. I do not want to be silent about "big" issues. This would be another form of tyranny. I do want to examine how the effects of education are variously experienced as inequities according to different participants in different sets of social and historical conditions. It is how difference is to be talked about—i.e., the creation of a more telling tale—that is the challenge for my own critique.

The big stories about teacher education have been created out of the languages that are made available in particular disciplinary fields or microcultures in the teacher education enterprise. They may be psychological stories, curriculum stories, sociological stories, management/leadership stories, policy stories, and so on. It could be claimed, then, that teacher education as a set of practices is in many important respects a discursive production. I recognize it, however, as invention that is always limited, partial, and open in explaining how things are and might be. In my own pedagogical work, I have been aware of how easy it is to be buffeted about by gusts of opinion that blow from different disciplinary landscapes, as though each alone would explain, disrupt, or save the world. The examination I undertake of the issue of improving teacher education practice is motivated by my own "struggle for pedagogies" (Gore, 1993), not my clarity about the truth of one or other of these competing discourses in teacher education. As a teacher educator, I am aware of the temptation to provide clarity for pre-service teachers by presenting my one political story rather than allowing them to do their own multiple reading of teaching stories in multiple ways.

THE AUTHOR AS A CRITICAL TEACHER EDUCATOR

I have been both a student teacher and a classroom teacher. I came to teacher education with 19 years teaching experience in secondary schools throughout Queensland, Australia. My motivations were many. Young people seemed to me to lack a sense of power and pedagogical energy in their work as pre-service and beginning teachers. They almost literally waved the white flag from day one. Whatever teacher educators thought they were doing that was relevant, I reasoned, their practices were drastically in need of overhauling, and I was, of course, just the one to do it. Now, as a teacher educator of five years standing, I am confronted by that very same critique of my own work, at least in theory, in the challenges made by experienced teachers enrolled in my postgraduate classes.

What has become evident to me in being a teacher educator is that teacher educators do not play as significant a role in the professional preparation of teachers as is popularly understood. As Hawley (1992) points out, the bulk of students' experience of teacher education programs is not pedagogical and professional studies but subject disciplines and perhaps a component of liberal arts (p. 252). University teachers who describe themselves as teacher educators usually belong to a subset of particular departments that are in themselves a minority subset of the teacher education program.

As an academic, I have worked in a radical educational foundations department with strong credentials in social critique. I soon learned that "teacher educator," whether critical or no, was not a label with much academic status attached to it in academic institutions. As a teacher educator, I was unlikely to receive much collegial support from academic peers who were inclined to regard teacher education as less than rigorous in its scholarship, and to regard education as a lower-order discipline. Nor could I expect support from the bulk of teachers, who were yet to be convinced that teacher educators actually work for the good of the profession. Academics, not teachers, have been the overwhelming beneficiaries of teacher education research (Tripp, 1990). Awkwardly wedged between these two worlds yet at home in neither, teacher educators still have few allies in defending the practices of initial teacher education.

I became part of a pedagogical tradition in which the dominant mode of delivery of educational services seems to be through the "dollops" principle. In essence, programs are constructed out of bits of theory, curriculum, or practicum, each jostling with the others for limited pedagogical space. In six years I have seen the demise of the foundational disciplines as educational "theory." Psychology, sociology, and philosophy have been doled out in increasingly small measure because more pedagogical territory was demanded for curriculum "basics" and fieldwork. The institutional logic appeared to be that all these disparate bits would come together as a coherent and more relevant professional experience when processed intelligently by student teachers. Failing this, in-servicing would later remediate the deficits suffered by the beginning teacher.

As the 1980s wore on, multidisciplinary and interdisciplinary marriages of convenience were seen to be increasingly necessary in professional and pedagogical studies at my university, as "theorists" struggled to maintain a foothold in initial teacher education courses. The fact that student teachers experienced Sociology and Philosophy as more theoretical than Psychology made it difficult to defend this shrinking pedagogical territory. Psychology maintained a stronger claim to practicality, because of a more recognizable language and a more legitimate profile in business and industry. Interdisciplinary compromises were struck. While there was potential here for a richer interrogation of classroom practices, these liaisons were never dangerous enough to challenge old modes of delivery. The effect of these compromises was that disciplinary monologues were delivered in parallel rather than interrogated differently.

This sort of tinkering did nothing to moderate growing dissent from outside teacher education. Outsiders demanded less theory and more real-world experiences. Many of my coworkers, particularly those committed to socially critical agendas, spent less and less energy on the increasingly vulnerable and apparently anemic initial teacher education project. They joined with colleagues from humanities in lamenting what seemed to be a general malaise in "liberal" courses that were considered low-status, low-demand programs in universities and colleges. The problem of the discursive representation of the university itself was less likely to be addressed (Graff, 1988, p. 10). They joined many of their colleagues in expressing concern with the "quality" of undergraduates, their lack of grammatical or conceptual literacy. This seems generally to take precedence over the problems college or university teachers have in communicating the university's role to students and the broader community.

Unfortunately, what were to us as teacher educators important struggles over pedagogical and professional empires were little more than in-house squabbles when scrutinized from any vantage point outside the university context. Whatever our disciplinary convictions, a more serious accusation would have profound ramifications for all professional preparation. The claim is that teacher educators are guilty of "producer capture" (Marginson, 1992, p. 13), holding on to the entire teacher education project at the taxpayers' and consumers' expense without producing the educational goods.

It is too easy to dismiss this claim as an anti-intellectual conspiracy against teacher educators in universities. It is also too easy to find reasons for deserting the initial teacher education project altogether in favor of something more academically trendy. My response as a teacher educator is to reexamine the tradition of critical teacher education by working both within and against its assumptions. As a feminist drawing on poststructuralist work for my own pedagogical understanding I have, as Harding (1990) terms it, "one foot in modernity and the other in the lands beyond" (p. 100). This straddling of agendas is necessary for reconstructing my role in teacher education, but tricky in terms of an appropriate ideological "physique." As someone who has always shunned any sort of gymnastics, I fear the damage that can be inflicted on the body of my own work, to say nothing of the extent to which my own ideological fitness for critique is exposed so starkly to others. Yet I must agree with Harding that our inquiry can and ought to aim at producing "less partial and perverse representations without having to assert the absolute, complete, universal or eternal adequacy" (p. 100) of such representations. In this new arena of contestations we must become aware that it is the very clarity of rules for generating pure positions that can lead to total(izing) rigidity.

TEACHER EDUCATION POLICY AND RADICAL CRITIQUE

Teacher education is a particular sort of language system. Student teachers, academics, supervising teachers, administrators, policy makers, students, are all contributors to this system. However, because it is historically and socially constituted, this language system does not invite all contributions equally nor does it represent all contributors equally. Participants in this system all struggle to be heard, to find semiotic space for saying it our way. We are resistant when we feel that our talk is being co-opted to serve ends we do not want to serve. Many versions of "relevant" teacher education are produced and contested in this way. These versions may be taken up and rearticulated by policy makers and others to accommodate desired educational trends and resist problematic ones.

While the language of teacher education policy remains open, this does not necessarily mean lively debate among the stakeholders about the purposes and practices of initial teacher education. Indeed, there is a high degree of sameness and predictability, as well as difference and discontinuity, in the linguistic constructions of "relevant" teacher education in policy documents that I have both accommodated and resisted as a teacher educator.

Stephen Ball's work allows examination of the discursive technologies that have been used to weave policy tales in the past. Ball's (1993) contemporary theorizing of educational policy permits a reconstructed critical reading of contemporary policy as discourse (p. 10).

He provides this corrective moment for policy analysis by insisting on the impossibility of single-theory explanations, given the complexity and scope of policy as sets of processes and outcomes. Ball argues:

> We cannot rule out certain forms and conceptions of social action simply because they seem awkward or theoretically challenging or difficult. The challenge is to relate together analytically the *ad hocery* of the macro with the *ad hocery* of the micro without losing sight of the systematic bases and effects of *ad hoc* social actions. (p. 10)

Ball acknowledges that much policy analysis emanating out of the modernist theoretical project is predictable in its format and its rhetoric. This is problematic if we are to accept the Foucauldian notion that "the relations of power are not in superstructural positions with merely a role of prohibition or accompaniment" but have "a directly productive role" (Foucault, 1981, cited in Ball, 1993, p. 13). The products are truths and knowledges as discourses—"practices that systematically form the objects of which they speak" (Foucault, 1972/1977, cited in Ball, 1993, p. 14). "The state" is likewise produced through discourse, "a point in the diagram of power" (Ball, 1993, p. 14) rather than a monolithic and sinister entity. The challenge, as Ball sees it, is to avoid both the "naive optimism" that focuses only on the possibilities for "secondary adjustments" to "policy ensembles" (including, for example, self-governance through "market, management appraisal and performativity") and the "naive pessimism" that denies the complexities and contradictions in the discursive arena of policy formulation and implementation (pp. 14–15).

Since the late 1980s, educational critical policy analysis has proliferated in keeping with a burgeoning volume of "official" educational policy. Many of the analyses may be held to be exemplars of the naive pessimism of which Ball speaks, yet most attempt to map problematic policy ensembles, in particular that of market, management appraisal, and performativity. The outcome is analysis that insists on a particular relationship between contemporary educational policy and a sovereign model of power.

This analysis is now well rehearsed. Simply put, the argument is that a new urgency has been brought to the relevance debate as a result of international economic uncertainty (Bates, 1992; Bowe, Ball, & Gold, 1992; Marginson, 1992; Peters & Marshall, 1989). We have been witnessing at an international level heightened concerns about the relationship of national economic decline to the quality of schooling, of teaching, and of teacher preparation. Since the mid-1980s western governments have been in crisis. Bates (1992, p. 2) argues that the crisis has four dimensions: third world insolvency, insolvency in western financial institutions, the economic problems of scaling down armaments for a post–Cold War United States, and the slowing of western economies, especially that of a reintegrating Germany. In an attempt to alleviate these problems, governments began to intervene in hitherto unprecedented ways in the work of higher education institutions in the name of greater accountability for diminishing resources. The driving logic is that education has a direct relationship to a postwelfare economy and that it can be manipulated to significantly affect productivity. Two mechanisms are at work here—the plundering of the nation state and the application of new technologies of production (Bates, 1992, pp. 3–4). In education, as in other areas of public endeavor, these mechanisms take the form of privatization and marketization.

This rationalizing has been manifest in a series of policy objectives and initiatives designed to bolster a more competitive economy through the privatization and commercialization of public sector activities *or* simulation of market activities within the public sector (Marginson, 1992). Combining economic rationalism and education has brought two different worlds into collision—a world of noncompetitive publicly subsidized uneconomic consumption and a world of competitive economic activity. What is of most concern is the flood of policy initiatives that seek inappropriately to turn educational and other public-sector institutions into market-sensitive corporations.

Critical analysts argue that these initiatives have remarkably similar ramifications for schooling and for teacher education throughout the western world. These have included a great sense of urgency in moves to reform teacher education in the 1980s and 1990s, so much so that reforming teacher education has been described as "a popular sport in the USA" (Hawley, 1992, p. 273) while similar claims have been made elsewhere.[1] According to Toomey (1989), teachers and academics have been called on to perform an education-led economic recovery. The logic to be resisted is that education is the key to economic growth and the work of educators is therefore in need of scrutiny for its inability to produce the goods. Porter's (1990) understanding of the driving logic is very clear indeed:

> The assumption is that students may be viewed as human capital, that teacher educators and teachers are basically trainers and that schooling should be seen primarily as an investment for a competitive national future. (p. 1)

Versions of the above analysis have been elaborated by critical policy analysts in the United States, Britain, New Zealand, and Australia as they examine moves to integrate industrial needs with economic policy. They claim that these have precipitated a series of critical shifts in pressures on and within teacher education in the name of accountability and in the context of diminishing resources (Bartlett, Knight, & Lingard, 1991; Bates, 1992; Bowe, Ball, & Gold, 1992; Lingard, 1991; Popkewitz, 1987; Tickle, 1987). Despite postmodern challenges to totalizing accounts of the relations between education and "the state," many of the tales told by educational sociologists about the education/economy interface still quite predictably identify and reiterate the dangers of "The Great Moving Right Show" (Hall, 1979).

The 1980s generated a huge volume of critical educational literature that examined the implications of all this for teacher educators. This literature had a very powerful effect on my understanding of myself as working in ways that are oppositional within the teacher education project. I understood myself as working against a dominant instrumentalist tradition by trying to "politicize" understandings of good teaching practice. And to do this, I drew on critiques that focused on both an "old order," based on behaviorist competency-based models of teaching, and a "new order," which further refined such technicist models in terms of industrial effectiveness. Such literature has been variously described as "reconceptualist curriculum theory" (Schubert, 1989), a "knowledge base reform movement" (Henderson, 1988), "reflective" (Gore, 1987), "avant garde" (Smith & Zantiotis, 1988a), or "critically reflective" (Elbaz, 1988). This range of terminology does indicate that these critiques of teacher education were neither a monolithic nor a unified body of literature. They are the work of diverse individual scholars (Shaker & Kridel, 1989) many of whom have refused categorization perhaps for somewhat the same reasons that Marx declared himself to be "not a Marxist." They understood the potential for marginalization and misrepresentation that such tags can bestow.

This literature contends that attempts to problematize the notion of "quality" teaching and the contexts in which it is embedded by studying themes such as language, history, culture, and power fell victim to global "rationalization" of teacher education programs in the mid-1980s (Liston & Zeichner, 1987, p. 34). According to Carr (1989), the "problem" of teacher quality was increasingly articulated through new technocratic and bureaucratic vocabularies that left many assumptions about learning and teaching unexamined. The anomaly between calls for greater teacher quality and on-going cutbacks to education was highlighted by analysts who then asked how seriously we should take this quality agenda (Toomey, 1989, p. 49).

In the United States, a "post *Nation-at-Risk*" era of critique emerged out of interventions in higher education that brought teacher education under special scrutiny (Shaker & Ullrich, 1987, p. 11). The "reductionist" tenor of reforms proposed by both the Carnegie Forum on Education and the Economy, *A Nation Prepared: Teachers for the Twenty-first Century* (1986), and the Holmes Group, *Tomorrow's Teachers* (1986), were perceived to connect higher education to no greater social purposes than those of serving the corporate demands of emerging economic conditions (Romanish, 1987).

Likewise, political interventions of a "sudden and rapid" nature (Tickle, 1987, p. 7) were identified in the United Kingdom. The Department of Education and Science White Paper *Teacher Quality* (1983) responded to a perceived decline in teacher competence and in schooling in general, by means of the creation of bureaucratic mechanisms such as the Council for the Accreditation of Teacher Education invoked in 1984 as a monitoring body for all teacher education courses. Concern was expressed by policy analysts in Britain about the interests served by the reassertion of state powers through the tightening of government control of agencies and institutions of learning and curriculum planning (Lawton, 1984; Salter & Tapper, 1981), and the reductionist versions of "quality" thereby produced.

The Education Reform Act, introduced in England and Wales in 1988, is still held responsible by critical policy analysts for fundamental and problematic changes in the cultures of schools as educational institutions and as managerial units (Bowe et al., 1992). Such developments are argued to signal an end to the relative progressivism of the Plowden Report (1967) and to herald a new era in which "raising standards" can only be conceived of in cost-effective terms. Two recent developments in the delivery of initial teacher education, the Licensed Teacher Scheme and the Articled Teacher Scheme, have been critiqued for their apparent relaxation of entry criteria, their failure to provide opportunity for student teacher "reflectivity," and their "more for less" economic rationale (Hextall, Lawn, Menter, Sidgwick, & Walker, 1991).

Maintaining the pessimistic tenor of critique, the work of the Hillcole Group (Hill, 1990) nevertheless brings forward for scrutiny some similarities as well as some differences in the playing out of new educational agendas in Britain and the United States. There are differences in the enactment of change, Hill (1990) argues, that can be attributed to differences in the politico-cultural development of these two trans-

Atlantic societies, Thatcherite Britain having a stronger tradition of counterideological organization than the Reagan and post-Reaganite United States. Nevertheless, Hill identifies similarities as including

> vocationalism, technicizing and deskilling of teaching; anti-egalitarianism; increased differentiation among schools, school students/pupils and teachers; the softening-up attack on teachers and their educators, and . . . tightened control over the school and the teacher curriculum. (p. 1)

Such trends were also identified in educational reform in New Zealand in the latter part of the 1980s. Lauder, Middleton, Boston, and Wylie (1988) spoke of a "third wave" of educational provision "dominated by New Right thinking . . . a retreat from achievement to ascription" (p. 16). Peters and Marshall (1989) agreed that "neoconservative" perspectives are the dominant theme of recent educational policy emanating from the New Zealand government. Further, they argued that the values of efficiency and competition have been driven more deeply into New Zealand's social fabric "at the expense of the values of liberal humanism—social-cultural equity and equality of opportunity" (p. 17).

The major overhauling of Australia's tertiary institutions in recent times has come in for similar criticism, although the strategy employed at the federal level has been identified as different from that in the United Kingdom or New Zealand, more *corporate managerialist* than *reprivatized* in character (Porter, Lingard, & Knight, 1991). This corporate strategy is held to have important ramifications for teacher educators in terms of pressure to narrow "relevant" curricula. Numerous national policy initiatives have been concerned with issues of "quality" or the lack of it in teacher education courses (Lingard, 1991). Concern has been expressed that the focus on teacher quality is driven by a policy agenda that locates teachers and teaching skill narrowly as objects of economic value (Bartlett et al., 1991). Reports such as *Teacher Quality: An Issues Paper* (Schools Council, 1989), *Teacher Education in Australia* (Australian Education Council, 1990), *Discipline Review of Teacher Education in Mathematics and Science* (Speedy, 1990, p. 4), made it quite explicit that too much theory and not enough practical is the historical and current malaise of teacher education. The recent shift to competency-based skills has meant a new generation of policy that seeks to redress this imbalance as a more general malaise of higher education. Finn (in AEC Review Committee, 1991), the Mayer Committee (1992), and in particular Carmichael (1992) were highly significant moments in the rhetorical shift from the *lucky* to the *clever* to the *capable* country. In essence, the proposition that has driven the competency-based movement in Australia is that a "more skills" cult will deliver a better future. Cairns (1992) describes the new wave of reform as "a cargo cult tinged with the work ethic" (p. 32).

What has been lacking in a great many analyses such as those briefly alluded to above is an assessment of the opportunities that situations that have been identified as "crises" can also generate for re-thinking our practices. In *Education and the Economy: Themes and Issues,* Jamieson (1989) elaborates on this point:

> There are two facets to the concept of crisis . . . danger and opportunity. The danger is there: economic collapse could sweep away or seriously damage much of the modern infrastructure of the Welfare State, education included. But opportunity is also there [for] a new flowering of debates about pedagogy, and a reorientation towards student centered, active and experiential learning. (p. 72)

This should mean neither retreat from change, nor naive acceptance of all reformations as improvement. To seek to return to old traditions by means of belated appeals to the disciplinary "dollop" model of teacher education *theory* is very tenuous indeed, if we accept the analysis of Battersby and Retallick (1988). They argue that a "maintenance orientation" in contemporary teacher education policy discourses militates against real movement away from what are constructed (often narrowly) as the "skills" of teaching, best achieved by models that move toward school settings and away from university settings. They claim that the rhetoric of teacher education has become so heavily psychologized that, while "the rudiments of human growth and development, learning and motivation" count as crucial in post-welfare constructions of a "relevant" agenda, "ideological, political and economic dimensions of education and schooling" do not (p. 11). *Theory,* by implication, is to be equated with a reconstructed educational/industrial/organizational psychology.

The 1990s need a more dynamic debate than that which characterized the 1980s. Policy analyses need to be more than the doppelgängers of postwelfare reforms. This means policy analysts must do more than generate "clear" stories about government interventions that divide debate simplistically on conventional political lines, i.e., a left/liberationist/antistatist stance versus a right-wing/populist/reprivatizing position. Hunter (1984) would go further, arguing that "top-down" analyses that warn against "the cunning power of the state bent on governing through a system of repressive tolerance" (p. 75) ought to give way to studies into the networks through which local changes in pedagogic, familial, and welfare institutions are made. He asserts that:

> Government, in the sense of the regulation of conduct and the attribution of social capacities, is not the prerogative of a state acting on behalf of deeper economic interests in relation to which the school and the family are mere instruments. (pp. 75–76)

The argument is that a single vantage point, that of "public intellectual," does not allow for addressing the complexity of education as an amalgam of "expert systems" (Hunter, 1992, p. 489). Thus clarity about the "state-as-adversary" can be a weakness rather than a strength. Attempts to set clear parameters in which matters of injustice ought to be identified in education is therefore as problematic as it is in any other area of social endeavor. The dubiousness of any claim to speak for others is certainly thrown into high relief when issues of race, sexuality, class, and gender intersect as they do so problematically in classrooms or in courtrooms. For example, in recent Thomas/Hill debates around the accusation made by an African-American man that an African-American woman had conspired to lynch him, no one could claim to voice the "true" perspective for African-Americans or for women. Any totalizing claim was vulnerable.

Unlearning privilege as academics or feminists or social critics is an important if daunting task. Refusing this is to leave intact our "clear images" about systems and our roles in them. We are complicit in the systems we purport to struggle against, despite the claims we might make to working oppositionally, outside and beyond *the* logic of *the* system. It has been as crucial and demanding a task for me as a teacher educator to acknowledge this as it continues to be for the pre-service teachers I work with.

This acknowledgment does not, unhappily, signal an end of injustice as a macro issue for all educators. Nor ought we give up on political critique in dealing with global or national issues. While Hunter (1984) urges studies of local networks, I believe that this need not be an either/or choice of grand *versus* small narratives, as long as stories that deal with macro issues are reflexive about the politics they seek to critique, and are perceptive about the disjunctions and disparities that are so inconvenient in mapping the big picture. "Big" does not have to mean all-embracing.

NEW ANALYSES, NEW LANGUAGE TOOLS

Given that "the field of practice is a broken and uneven place" (Spivak, cited in Lather, 1993, p. 3), opportunities must be generated by teacher educators and others to establish and explore links between the discursive practices of academics, policy makers, and practitioners as arenas of daily struggle. I have been heartened by what feminist poststructural endeavor can contribute to my own understanding of the struggle to articulate teacher education as sets of practices that respond to the educational needs of pre-service teachers and their future students. Importantly, feminist poststructural work focuses on the politicized and politicizing nature of the talk that abounds in any site on which versions of relevance/appropriateness struggle for legitimacy. This demands that the neatness and the clarity of a single paradigm or disciplinary voice developed in linear fashion be surrendered in favor of untidiness and fragmentation. Rather than attempt to tease apart or untangle networks of ideas, the challenge is to analyze contingent or haphazard sets of relationships. In teacher education policy, this means attending to the effects of policy reform as a language system. This involves examining the ways in which notions like *relevance* are articulated, disarticulated, and rearticulated by and for a range of publics.

Nancy Fraser's (1989) analysis of welfare discourse, *Unruly Practices: Power, Discourse and Gender in Contemporary Social Theory,* is very useful for this purpose. Fraser draws on the insights of Foucault, French deconstructionists, Rorty, and Habermas to develop an integrated "politics of need interpretation" that has a practical intent of social change (p. 7). What is most important about her work is that she tries to analyze social inequity without using the simplistic dichotomies that deny cultural multiplicity. This makes possible a more telling analysis than the old "state versus us" rhetoric.

Fraser (1989) strives to identify the roles of human agency, social conflict, and the construction and deconstruction of social meanings in the whole arena of welfare-state conflict, defined as "the struggle over needs" (p. 10). Before attempting to draw parallels between the struggle to define welfare needs as analyzed by Fraser, and the struggle to define education needs, I will briefly outline some contributions Fraser has made to a contemporary understanding of the notion of social struggle, because I seek to apply her linguistic tools to teacher education policy.

While Fraser (1989) does not desert a critical agenda, she refuses traditional Leftist academic analyses in favor of "a genre of critical theorizing that blends normative argument and empirical sociocultural analysis in 'a diagnosis of the times'" (p. 6). With the aim of disclosing some specifically late capitalist forms of male dominance, she problematizes uncontested gender-based dichotomies: "domestic as distinct from economic," "home as distinct from work," "mother as distinct from breadwinner." Her particular focus is on interpretations of women's welfare needs and the role of these interpretations in the constitution of social identities (p. 10).

For Fraser (1989), needs discourses are "political" when a particular matter "is contested across a range of different discursive arenas and among a range of different discursive publics" (p. 167). The political, then, in Fraser's terms, denies the separateness of categories like "cultural," "private," "domestic," "economic," "personal" (p. 6). The Marxist notion of social struggle is reworked as struggles for cultural *hegemony*—the power to construct and articulate authoritative definitions of social situations and legitimate interpretations of needs (p. 6).

Importantly for my reconstructed tale as a political narrative, Fraser uses the terms "politics" and "political" in more than one sense. She speaks of an institutional sense ("official political") and a discursive sense ("politicized") that are related because legitimation usually follows "debate across a wide range of discourse publics" (p. 166). "Publics," according to Fraser, can be distinguished along a number of axes, which may be ideological (e.g., political party allegiance), stratified (e.g., gender, class), "issue-based" (e.g., environmentalists), "power-based" (e.g., elite enclaves, large authoritative groups, small poorly resourced enclaves), and so on (p. 167). Fraser's connotation of "politicized talk," then, is contestation through a wide range of forms of articulation, including formal and informal speech and writing. She argues that official political discourse functions in general to depoliticize particular contestations by "economizing" them so that "the issues in question . . . are cast as impersonal market imperatives, as 'private' ownership prerogatives, or as technical problems for managers and planners, all in contradistinction to political matters" (p. 168).

In this framework, Fraser analyzes contested talk over the issue of needs that ought to be met by welfare services. The analysis provided by Fraser of the processes of articulation of welfare needs in late capitalist societies provides a map that delineates the lines or axes along which *needs discourses* compete (p. 171). Social struggle is not only between politicized *oppositional needs talk* and the *reprivatization needs talk* of powerful organizational interests bent on shaping "hegemonic needs interpretation," but also between oppositional needs talk and expert needs talk in and around the social state. These encounters in turn define additional axes of struggle that are highly complex, because various social groups will continue to seek state provision, yet may well seek to resist particular administrative and institutional needs interpretations.

What Fraser stresses in her analysis of the struggle to articulate welfare needs is discursive interrelatedness. Her focus is on a precarious and impure terrain of fragmentations and contestations, rather than on clear class divisions. Nevertheless, she does attempt to account for some discursive struggles by analyzing relationships along particular axes. Reprivatization needs talk, for example, is linked to oppositional needs talk in more complex ways than a simple rejection of the call for more social-welfare services. Reprivatization discourses respond to oppositional needs talk in that they continue to articulate entrenched needs interpretations but at the same time modify these. Fraser provides the example of British Thatcherism, where reprivatization discourses articulated through authoritarian populism "shaped the subjectivities of a wide range of disaffected constituencies and united them in a powerful coalition" (p. 173). A more recent American example would be the way in which President Bush was heralded a popular hero during the Gulf War, a war that redirected vital funds away from the domestic needs of those very constituents who applauded his role.

While oppositional and reprivatization needs discourse, then, can define an axis of needs struggle, a second line of conflict is identified by Fraser for which the central issue is the interpreted *content* of contested needs "once their political status has been successfully secured" (p. 173). In the contexts of social problem solving, institution building, and professional class formation, forms of expert needs talk are generated and become the vehicles for translating sufficiently politicized needs into "objects of potential state intervention" (p. 173). These expert needs discourses tend to be restricted to specialized publics such as university academics through expert vocabularies and rhetorics.

Fraser's analysis of how the multiplicity of types of needs talk generated by and for a number of different publics continues to be recreated and contested in the highly political struggle to define welfare needs is most applicable to analysis of struggles over what is needed from teacher education. Initial teacher education may be regarded as a form of social welfare in that it makes large financial demands on the public purse, and as such is subject to constant scrutiny about whether it is achieving the "right" objectives. Like welfare work, the work of teacher educators is a type of politics "in which the 'truth' [about schools and teaching] is produced and contested" (Smith &

Zantiotis, 1988b, p. 83). And like welfare work, these discursive versions of appropriate practice are neither fixed nor pure, but are constantly shifting, accommodating, resisting, threatening to collapse, and being shored up by a variety of publics.

I have co-opted the three major kinds of politicized interpretations of needs that Fraser (1989, p. 171) identifies in late capitalist welfare discourse—oppositional, reprivatization, and expert—as a framework to analyze the needs talk that is generated about the preparation of teachers. Given that my own commitment as a teacher educator has been formed out of social reconstructionist and feminist scholarship, the temptation to situate myself as an oppositional voice is strong. However, a more reflexive tale unfolds when I displace critical traditions from their self-appointed oppositional location and probe them as expert talk, no more or less complicit in the successes and failures of teacher education programs than any other academic voices.

The problems in constructing macro-analyses of policy become more evident when Fraser's framework is applied to analyses of "official political" articulations of relevant teacher education. The lack of purity of all competing discourses becomes apparent. Fragments of liberal-progressive expert and radical oppositional talk will be recuperated, accommodated, and conflated with free market or reprivatization talk, despite the possible intention of opposition. If we are to accept Fraser's analysis, this can sometimes happen in quite predictable ways that allow commonalities to be identified across particular exemplars of official political talk. In teacher education this could be said to occur in the "market, management appraisal and performativity policy ensembles" of which Stephen Ball (1993) speaks. The expertise of academics as "public intellectuals" is likewise an amalgam of talk that may indeed be less representative of oppositional voices than its own rhetoric allows. What is so galling for critical analysts is the way that vocabularies that began as a closed system of bottom-up resistance (terms like "empowerment," "participation," "collegiality") seem to be quickly co-opted to agendas that are apparently managerial and prescriptive.

Smyth's (1991) analysis of "contrived collegiality" in reforming the teaching profession (p. 338) provides an example of this concern in critical work. Smyth (1991, p. 337) argues that there is a resurgence of the idea that to act professionally is to act in partnership with the state. Citing such "progressive" schemes as the Pittsburgh Teacher Professionalism Project, he asserts that, far from enhancing teacher collegiality, schemes like this put teachers in danger of becoming "agents charged with policing one another's oppression" (p. 338). The point is that the "emancipation" rhetoric surrounding these schemes, e.g., "Teachers are switching from order-takers to decision-makers" (*New York Times*, May 2, 1990, cited in Smyth, 1991, p. 338), is a powerful means of sustaining the claims of project administrators to the professed goal of devolution, not surveillance.

TEACHER EDUCATION POLICY AS A DISCURSIVE STRUGGLE

The fact that there are struggles to articulate *the* version of a particular area that is deemed ripe for contesting means that competing definitions must abound, with policy writers and analysts understanding the importance of stealing a linguistic march on their perceived opposition. What is important in official discourse is to occupy the high moral ground by colonizing "good" terminology—e.g., competence, quality, excellence (see Wolin [1983] for a decade-old discussion still relevant today). There is great difficulty in launching the sorts of critiques sketched out briefly above when resistance to a market-driven agenda looks so much like a stand against all that might well be regarded as positive. Critique of any stated position or policy is, by implication, dubious when it apparently refuses such patently good choices as competence or quality in favor, presumably, of incompetence, lack of quality, and so on. Accusations that academics and other critics are more motivated by fear of scrutiny into their own shoddy practices than by other, more noble, goals can be made to stick.

"What are they trying to hide?" may become both a catchphrase and a rallying point, as individuals in a very broad range of publics who are disaffected by educational institutions unite in the politics of the backlash. Implicit in "What are they hiding?" is the proposition that "They have been caught out." An editorial published in the British newspaper the *Sunday Telegraph* (January 5, 1992) is an example of this. It applauds a "reading recovery" scheme planned by the British Conservative government that will involve, among other benefits, a radical relocation of teacher training into schools, reworking official discourse into a powerful piece of populist discourse about teacher education:

> Institutions of teacher training have for 20 years or more been dominated by anti-educational ideologies, by child-centred methods in general and egalitarian dogmas in particular. . . . The way to break the hold of these dogmas is to put teacher training in the hands of practising teachers and remove it from the grip of sociological and political theorists. . . . We are . . . to have a system of teacher training

based on what is in effect a demarcation of good schools from bad schools. It is right that this should be so: no sensible industry would base the training of its workforce in bad factories. . . . The system of enforced levelling down in education is thus about to be replaced by one dominated by clearly recognisable standards of excellence and by competition to meet them. . . . At a time when the gap in standards between the independent and maintained sectors is growing, only the doctrinaire or the niggardly would fail to welcome such a development.

What I want to focus on briefly here is not the "content" but the reworking of equality negatively as "egalitarian *dogma*" and "enforced levelling down." "Recognisable standards of excellence" are constructed as standing in opposition to equality as "forced-levelling-down." Egalitarianism is reconstructed as the impediment to, not the social goal of, teacher education.

I have noted elsewhere the significance of setting up linguistic versions of *equality* that are clearly to be pitted against *liberty*, including the freedom to be "excellent" (McWilliam, 1987). In the above editorial, the call that is characteristic of reprivatization talk—i.e., to increase the "independent" sector at the expense of the "maintained"—depends on this dichotomizing of *excellence* and *equality*. However, it is more than a simple juxtaposition of these terms in any one document, official or otherwise, that is the issue here. It is the impurity of sets of practices that can both eschew and embrace equality, e.g., through the level-playing-field rhetoric of the "market/management/performativity policy ensembles" of which Stephen Ball (1993) speaks.

I would argue that, in reprivatization discourse in Australia, there is an apparently greater commitment to the rhetoric of "equality-as-equity" than there is in Britain, the result in part of the unprecedented success of Labor governments in holding office in recent decades. However, it is interesting to note the more subtle shift, in harsher economic times, from versions of equity as *affirmative action* or *positive discrimination* to equity as wastage of potential talent for labor. Cultural difference as disadvantage is reworked as "skill deficits" that need to be overcome by more intensive and relevant vocational training (Knight, McWilliam, & Bartlett, 1993).

The struggle to define "reflectivity" in the teacher education literature of the 1980s and early 1990s is another interesting example of this phenomenon. Once there is broad consensus that reflective teachers are better teachers, then the struggle to articulate versions of this contested term becomes more energized, more vociferous. Energy for the debate has dissipated as the terrain of contestation shifts to more urgent sites of struggle (e.g., standards). *Reflectivity* was an important site of contestation within the expert discourses of academe before it began to see the linguistic light of day in the official discourse of teacher education policy documents. The phrase "reflective teaching," indeed, became "part of the language of teacher education" in the 1980s (Gore, 1987, p. 33), so much so that some critics sounded a note of warning that "reflection" was "on the brink of becoming ambiguous, if it has not already joined the ranks of educational catchwords" (Munby & Russell, 1989, p. 76). The sheer volume of teacher education literature that makes use of the term, regardless of disciplinary or ideological orientation, is testimony to this.

As the terms "reflective" and "critically reflective" became increasingly pervasive in teacher education discourse, problems of competing definitions, devaluation, and appropriation abounded. Some definitions, in fact, appeared to stand in direct contradiction to others. Cruickshank and Applegate's (1981) reflective teaching approach, for example, in its emphasis on a controlled teaching experience as providing the opportunity for thoughtful pre-service teacher analysis, differed markedly from that of Zeichner (1981–82) and Korthagen (1985), both of whom were critical of the Cruickshank model as technocratic and positivistic. Ross and Hannay (1986) expressed the same reservations about Beyer's (1979, 1984a, 1984b) work. The work of Shulman (1987), which now permeates much official discourse about teacher education, met a similar fate with many critical theorists (see, for example, Sockett, 1987). It has been critiqued as "working within technocratic rationality as a model of knowledge production and its use" (Munby & Russell, 1989, p. 76). Shulman's definition of reflection as "what a teacher does when he or she looks back at the teaching and learning that has occurred, and reconstructs, re-enacts and/or recaptures the events, emotions and the accomplishments" (1987, p. 19), has been discounted as a-contextual and uncritical (Valli & Tom, 1988).

Debate has not been limited to the extent to which a particular model or theory fell within or outside the parameters of critical reflectivity. It has also existed within "critical" expert discourses about ways reflective inquiry might be facilitated in actual teacher education programs (Wildman & Niles, 1987). Some, like Ross and Hannay (1986), expressed a rather negative view of the possibilities for a working model of critically reflective practice, criticizing academics who preach the value of inquiry instruction while using traditional exposition in their own classrooms. Others, like Grumet (1989a), have been more hopeful, looking to political and community models, such as the aesthetic model of studio education used by practitioners in the arts, as an appropriate pedagogical model.

Just as reflectivity has become exhausted by the energy spent on its appropriation, so too has the term "action research." Once the darling of the educationally daring, action research has had strong enough factory-floor credentials to make it very worthy of contestation and appropriation for a range of projects that might be loosely termed "workplace restructuring." A leading advocate of action research as emancipatory educational work in the 1980s, Stephen Kemmis (1991) speaks of the inevitability of this contestation, and of his now being at odds with a number of contemporary advocates of action research. He is particularly critical of way action research has been co-opted to generate new forms of organizational development in corporate capitalism and to serve radical rationalist reconstructions of the machinery of schooling. The point here is not that action research got it wrong methodologically or ideologically, but that the language of action research itself has been no more fixed or limitless than any other language because it emanates from advocates of social change from below. What is noteworthy is the ripeness of democratic discourses such as these for recuperation as slogans of reprivatization talk, and the speed with which these linguistic processes occur. Robin McTaggart (1991a), a staunch advocate of participatory models of research, has commented on his disappointment with the "technicisation of action research" and the danger of "its confusion with political activism" (p. 46). Its potential to act as a form of cultural imperialism for Aboriginal people in Australia cannot be separated from its "good credentials" in cross-cultural education, but depends on this very reputation.

SO WHAT?

For the contemporary critical teacher educator as the subject of educational policy discourse, three key issues are raised out of analyses like these.

First, matters pertaining to the relationship between social justice and education are not diminished according to the degree of sophistication of academic debate, just as they are not diminished by the extent to which policy makers lay claim to moral high ground or to factory-floor pragmatism (the latter, of course, being continuously reworked as synonymous with the former position).

Second, there is no language system that can be put in place to permanently serve as an inexorable march toward social justice. The very fact that "politically correct" is a term now used to bury critical projects rather than to praise them certainly bears this out.

Third, coping with uncertainty means more complex challenges than identifying flaws in the projects of others. Critical teacher educators are always complicit in the very discursive system we purport to resist. Recognition of this has already meant, for feminists in particular, exploring new ways of writing educational texts as we grapple with pedagogical possibilities beyond poststructuralism. It must also mean, in teacher education, that we move beyond the "clear images" in which debate has been conducted on the familiar terrain of teacher education policy as folklore. In pursuing better educational practice for ourselves and our students, we must acknowledge and confront the partiality of our own stories and their potential for surveillance and repression. And to do this, we must keep generating new strategies for storytelling, not continue to rely on old plots.

CHAPTER 2

In Broken Images

Feminisms of Difference for Teacher Education Research

A CRITIQUE OF THE CRITICS

At the end of the 1980s, Michael Apple (1988) reminded critical scholars that "clarity begins at home" (p. 204). It was a caution against obscurity in critical scholarship. Apple warned of the need for scholars to recognize the political issues around the languages of critical scholarship and their potential for reproducing the unequal social relations such writers purport to oppose. In the light of the previous chapter, I would argue that this reworking of the old aphorism might signal a problematic that is more than merely a message about the state of academic prose. It might also caution us against the "blissful clarity"[1] that is the result of keeping our familiar discourses intact.

Critical traditions of scholarship have relied heavily on "us-versus-them" oppositions. Breaking with these simplistic ways of seeing ourselves and others is difficult, especially when the images of ourselves that are reflected back to authors are seductively self-sustaining. Unmasking the conspiracy makes the writer the hero of the story. So it is much easier, having invested heavily in our own discursive practices, to diminish contrary views than to generate reflexive moments for ourselves. This may well account for a certain predictability in critical scholarship, an at times overwhelming preference for critique that reiterates what is wrong without moving on to articulate the possible. Meanwhile, critique as on-site practice is left to others to enact. Among these "others" are significant numbers of beginning teachers.

As a teacher educator, I locate myself in a tradition of critical scholarship but I acknowledge that this tradition does not seem to have an impressive record of preparing socially critical teachers, whatever the arguments that might be mounted about the difficulties of "raising

critical consciousness." Teacher educators who have conducted research that works against relations of dominance have faced a "black
hole" in critical theory—a lack of knowledge regarding the conditions
that must be met if people are going to be in a position to actually
consider using critical theory as a possible account of their lives (Fay,
1977, p. 218). A tradition of evangelizing in initial teacher education
must be challenged in ways that do not romanticize critical educators
or their students. And a crucial first step is to understand educational
research as not separate from but integrated with those practices. This
means proceeding somewhat differently from the dominant patterns
of tertiary work, in which the bifurcation of research and teaching is
usually quite explicit, with research hierarchically positioned over and
above teaching. It involves a much more egalitarian reworking of this
relationship through practices that forge links for research-as-praxis
(Lather, 1986). In turn, this allows certain strategic interventions into
initial teacher education of a kind that open up possibilities for "saying
it otherwise" in discursively constructing resistance to Eurocentrism,
classism, sexism, racism, and other forms of difference.

The tale that follows takes up the challenge of telling research in
ways that do not seek to "tidy" difference but to display it. This requires vocabularies that differ at times from predictable teacher education discourse. The quest for doing it differently yet saying it the
same—i.e., remaining in the comfort zone of a familiar language system—is an impossible one. While "quantitative" is instantly recognizable as a "legitimate" word in any mainstream discussion of teacher
education research, "semiotics" is not. To return to Apple's (1988)
point, the challenge is to give access to new knowledges and debates,
not to generate simplistic versions of theory that end in misrepresentation.

TEACHER EDUCATION RESEARCH:
THE NEED TO MAKE THE BREAK

I want to explore the possibility of doing different teacher education research, by examining what feminist poststructuralist theory
might contribute to educational research methodology. This tale, therefore, stands in opposition to stories told by self-styled pragmatists who
would reconstruct teacher education as an anti-intellectual project of
the "hands on, minds off" variety. (Mention has been made in Chapter
1 of this as a theme of much current teacher education policy.) It also
is written against the logic of those who are saying and doing more of

the same old "studying down" on pre-service teachers, regardless of the extent to which they call their inquiry qualitative or quantitative, or their discipline psychology or sociology. I write drawing on New French Theory, mediated by critical feminism. And I write because it is my belief that such theorizing, when applied to teacher education research, generates more engaging possibilities than the positivist cul-de-sac of mainstream research.

Over a decade ago, Bernstein (1983) stated:

> There is no knowledge without preconceptions and prejudices. The task is not to remove all such preconceptions, but to test them critically in the course of inquiry. (p. 128)

Such a challenge to the objectivism of social science would not be new to those with any interest in contemporary scholarship. Nevertheless, it is still disconcerting in its implications for valid research. Summaries of teacher education research such as that provided by Tisher and Wideen (1990) indicate that researchers are not inventing ways of working out of more slippery conceptualizations of validity, preferring the solidity of positivist assumptions. Knowledge as a base, as fixed, as "out there" waiting to be discovered and revealed as "findings," is a more comforting rationale for engaging in research activity. It is certainly seen as preferable to suffering the bouts of epistemological nervousness that the postmodern propensity for unsettling can cause. So it is understandable, if disappointing, that feminism, Foucault, or even French might be well and truly "F" words in the vocabulary of researchers who simply want to get the job done.

Nevertheless, educational research in general, and teacher education research in particular, continues to be challenged to move beyond the comfort zone of its "reductionist tendencies and barren methodological orthodoxy" (Lather, 1991a, p. 26). Traditional forms of educational research, i.e., empirical/analytical and historical/hermeneutic styles, have been under this sort of attack for some time. It has been argued that educational problems have been transformed, in the research process, into academic or technical ones and this is a result of the rational scientific premises on which so much educational research depends (Walker, 1985, p. 6). This concern has underpinned the search for new directions and new dimensions in pre-service teacher education inquiry, variously described as a movement toward pluralistic (Bertaux & Kohli, 1984; Tisher & Wideen, 1990), "inquiry-guided" (Mishler, 1990), or "multiple methods" research (Walker, 1985).

In an intellectual context that has moved "beyond objectivism and relativism" to critique the very idea of Method (Bernstein, 1983, p. xi), old quantitative-versus-qualitative debates are under pressure to give way to new methodological challenges. For any sort of contemporary social inquiry, such challenges would have researchers working in ways for which there are no methodological blueprints. For the teacher education researcher all this is seductively and depressingly lacking in prescription. The issue is particularly problematic for advocacy-oriented researchers whose work is usually conducted in response to a particular set of local conditions. Little wonder, given the degree of difficulty of working this way, that advocacy research has remained something of an oxymoron (Lather, 1989, p. 11).

The call to critical social scientific inquiry is a call to advocacy in the sense that it is a call to actively resist those forms of social life that perpetuate injustice (Carr & Kemmis, 1986; Kemmis, 1988. The call itself has not been diminished by "unorthodox" social theorizing, although action research is no longer left carrying the can of "radical orthodoxy" as the ideologically pure research method to have when you are not having a "method."

For critical educational researchers, a priority continues to be exploration of the dilemmas that have been articulated as a "theory/practice rift" in education. Their agendas have demanded of researchers forms of inquiry that seek to change rather than merely interpret the social world of learning and teaching. However, problems develop when the "truths" of a liberatory agenda are postulated without sufficient awareness of the ways in which all "systems of truth" involve a dispensation of those who can speak the truth and those who are subject to it (Rose, 1990, p. 4). Probing this further means addressing in particular the development of new languages for speaking about *subjectivity* and how they might both construct and deconstruct the language of research.

The use of the term "subjectivity" is highly significant for educational researchers because it signals a shift from understanding "persons" as coherent, rational, and unitary individuals to understanding them as fragmented, contradictory, and multiple "subjects." The preference for the term "subject" over "individual" and "subjectivity" over "individuality" indicates theoretical approaches that emphasize the way in which the social domain constitutes human "being" within it, rather than vice versa. Against the notion of "an irreducible humanist essence," much contemporary social theorizing assumes a subjectivity that is precarious, contradictory, and constantly in the process of reconstitution through discourse (Weedon, 1987, p. 33). This challenges statements about the teacher's role that have become the truisms of teacher education: "cater to individual needs," "help individuals reach their full potential," or "raise an individual's self-esteem." "Culture" as "society" as "context" is peripheral, garnish to the "individuality" roast.

Henriques and associates' notion of the importance of reconceptualizing the individual as *subject* is useful here (Henriques, Holloway, Urwin, Venn, & Walkerdine, 1984a). They argue that positing a "unitary psychological being" or "a rational intentional being" as a point of origin in social inquiry disallows the recognition of the way "selves" are socially constituted (p. 24). The theoretical correlate of this, they assert, is an "individual/society" dualism that constrains explanations of social behaviors and practices (p. 12). Their project seeks to unsettle psychology's individual/society dualism in order to overcome "the virtual impossibility of thinking outside the terms generated by the dualism" (p. 14). Holloway (1984) argues that this individual/society dualism has the effect of privileging the individual as the focus of various organizational activities, ignoring the social and power relations of institutions that constitute and thereby constrain "selves" as subjectivities (p. 56).

Reaction to this phenomenon in radical critiques has been, according to Henriques and associates (1984b, p. 91), to overcompensate by focusing on the transformation of "society" without recognizing the question of the place and the importance of changing subjects in relation to that social transformation. The monolithic and unitary notions of the nature of power that are characteristic of Marxist functionalist and structuralist analyses of the social domain are as inadequate to deal with the issue of changing subjects/subjectivities as are those of individuality.

Radical critics can no longer sustain either the idea that psychology reduces to sociology (Miller, 1990, p. 123), or that discourse is something wholly objective and external to subjects (p. 120). Henriques and associates (1984a) argue that an appropriate way forward is through debate that focuses on understanding and transforming subjectivity, a debate that privileges neither society nor individual as a starting point to understanding "the socially produced individual" (p. 9). The subject is a player in the game, not just a pawn (Miller, 1990, p. 123).

For the contemporary educational researcher, research that successfully engages with *difference* must be research that engages with some of the multiple, active, and dynamic subjectivities of the research participants. This demands much more complex metaphors of social research than, say, connecting with a moving target. If, as MacIntyre

(1984) asserts, "the problem with real life is that moving one's knight to QB3 may always be replied to with a lob across the net" (p. 98), then the limits of contemporary research design must be acknowledged. Designs must be generated that are flexible enough both to incorporate and to transcend modernist approaches that depend so much on rationalist logic (such as the quantitative/qualitative binary formulation of research methodology itself) for investigating the unitary individual or society.

Because research is inquiry made public, any new ways educators develop for presenting educational research must be coherent and accessible to other stakeholders in the education project. Teacher education can be no exception. Yet this ought not to be understood as synonymous with research that is one-dimensional, unimaginative, and rigid (Tesch, 1989, p. 62). Nor should it be understood any longer as straitjacketed by rationalist assumptions about the nature of valid inquiry. What it does require, given the challenge to be disinterested, value-free knowledge, is much greater attention to the "politics of method" (Eisner, 1988), that is, to the relations of power in the framing of the language of research and in the research act itself. "Who gets to say what about whom and why?" has now become a central question for the educational researcher (Tripp, 1990, p. 64). As I argued in the previous chapter, this is a particularly crucial question for those who understand themselves to be doing enabling educational work as researchers and teachers.

THE CHALLENGE OF *POSTPOSITIVIST* RESEARCH

Many contemporary feminists have assisted in mapping a new terrain of potentially fruitful social research by drawing on both modernist and postmodernist theorizing to rework educational research as a *postpositivist* activity (Lather, 1991a, p. 6). That means working from the logic of *postrationalist* assumptions about the nature of knowledge (Di Stephano, 1990, p. 67), not from logic that sets quantitative against qualitative as the either/or of legitimate inquiry. The break is not with rationalism. It is a break with the association of what is rational with a configuration of the subject as autonomous, implicitly male, neutral, contextless, and transcendental (Poster, 1989, p. 5). Consequently, the call for a different relationship of educational research to critical teaching is not a reiteration of the "progressive" call for more qualitative studies, greater eclecticism, or simply for more "peopled" research practices, such as might be presumed of action researchers. The aim is to signal ways of saying and doing teacher education more power-fully by *telling* teacher education research differently.

If knowledge is "produced" rather than "given" as *content* (Wex-ler, 1987, pp. 98–120), issues of context can no longer be regarded as peripheral to the research act. Instead, they become integral to an emergent focus on multiple realities. As Beyer (1988) describes it, "truth becomes supplanted by 'warranted assertability', knowledge by judgment and a-historicism by social and cultural context/valuation" (p. 80). This means that new work is both more tentative and more provocative as the focus shifts from prediction and prescription to dis-closure and deconstruction.

These challenges for research processes are providing new in-sights for educational inquiry. Not only are they generating perceptive critiques of what have stood for some time as definitive studies; they are also serving educators in drawing attention to how, as teacher edu-cators, we become reinscribed through our practices in the very poli-tics of truth[2] that we might claim to oppose (Gore, 1991, p. 48). New contextualized models of self-reflexive inquiry can help us as teacher educators to discover "what it is we have been incorporated into and what it is we have been unable to ask" (Sholle, cited in Lather, 1989, p. 10).

Contemporary epistemic challenges to modes of inquiry are not, therefore, a simple turning away from positivism, but also from the antipositivist, anti-empiricist impetus that has animated critical mod-ernism, particularly Marxist analyses. As "the dominant epistemic faiths of the modern period," both positivism and its doppelgänger Marxism have dissolved as oppositions (Hebdidge, 1988, p. 192). "Postpositivisms" as *postmodernist* phenomena represent a challenge to "any epistemological vantage point claiming totalistic knowledge" (Jay, 1988, p. 5). Master narratives have given way to a preoccupation with mirrors, icons, and surfaces (Hebdidge, 1988, p. 192).

Debate continues as to how to characterize the postmodern. As an intellectual phenomenon, it has been the subject of a vast and daunting array of analyses in the 1980s and 1990s. Debates continue to rage as to its inherent conservatism and/or antipolitical nature (e.g., Gill, 1991; Nicholson, 1990). For Connor (1989, p. 20), it is these very debates that constitute postmodernism as a phenomenon. While my concerns are informed from these debates to some extent, I do not purport to ad-dress this issue in any detail. It is the way feminists have engaged in and critiqued modern/postmodern debates, and the implications of this intellectual ferment for teacher education research, that is of inter-est here.

Whether postmodern or not, there is little doubt that new agendas have been emerging for some time in the humanities, and that these indicate major shifts in the objects of inquiry. Along with the burgeoning interest in the sociology of culture rather than structural analysis or humanistic evaluation, there has been a shift of emphasis from the author to the text as the vehicle of hegemonic values (den Hartog & Alomes, 1991, p. 9). The impetus for this reorientation has come in particular from a new generation of theory—*poststructuralism*. For this reason I want to examine briefly the contribution poststructuralism as "after" rather than "anti" structuralism has made to my own understanding of educational research.

Despite rejection of any unifying definition, French poststructuralist theorizing—evident in the works of Michel Foucault, Jean Baudrillard, Jacques Derrida, Gilles Deleuze, Jacques Lacan, Jean-François Lyotard—informs and is informed by postmodernist cultural logic, in its rejection of the formalism of structural linguistics and its challenges to the modernist assumptions of a coherent rational self. Poststructuralism informs current educational research by its active interruption of the totalizing narratives of modernist discourses, including psychologism and structural functionalism. It replaces their assumptions of coherence, clarity, and congealment with contrary assumptions of fragmentation, ferment, and fluidity. In this way, poststructuralism has added impetus to a disciplinary redefinition. It has enabled more sophisticated attempts to "replough familiar academic fields" (den Hartog & Alomes, 1991, p. 15) through forms of research that analyze written and spoken "texts" to inquire into the complexity of contemporary culture.

Den Hartog and Alomes (1991) sound a note of warning about the assumption that "all the world's a text" and the possibility that this can become "an excuse for solid empirical research when this is undoubtedly necessary" (p. 15). The strength of a postpositivist mode of inquiry is that these two forms of inquiry need not be pitted against each other. Researchers can proceed in ways that seek to utilize the best of both. Grumet (1989b) also warns against analysis of curriculum as text rather than as event, arguing that "the teacher is not exiled from the world she creates as the writer is" (p. 17). While still constrained as institutionally constituted subjects, teachers do have agency to change what happens in their classrooms as it transpires. Curriculum analysis must respond to the agency teachers have that writers, having written, do not.

Poststructuralist theory redirects researcher attention to the "broken" and "breaking" images of language as it actively constitutes and transforms the social world of participants in the teacher preparation process. Researchers are being challenged to look for more telling explanations of their struggle for meaning and the formation of their subjectivities (McLaren, 1988, p. 3). In asserting this, researchers can challenge the usefulness of those structuralisms too firmly rooted in causal determinism or simply too unspecified.[3] Yet, as critical researchers, we must not at the same time ignore the workings of real patterns of domination. An important issue was raised here for me as researcher/pedagogue. Could structuralist *and* poststructuralist theorizing inform the same study without raising serious epistemological, evidentiary, and political-ethical problems and so impair the coherence of the knowledge produced by the research? Surely the theoretical framework of such a research task could not derive from two sets of assumptions that are antithetical. Could the "scientific" assumptions of Althusser, for example, "nestle in" with the "arbitrariness" of Derrida or the "ambiguity" of Foucault? Or would their contrary assumptions disallow coherence? Other feminist scholars have put a great deal of work into attempting to come to grips with these same questions. In my own teacher education research, I felt that failure to grapple with these issues would make much more likely either a slide into relativism or an inflexible insistence that my vantage point was *the* vantage point.

FRENCH THEORY, FEMINISM, AND EDUCATIONAL RESEARCH

Because the contributions made by the structuralist Louis Althusser are important precursors to current critical feminist theory, I wanted to see how they might inform my own understanding of preservice teachers as subjects. Althusser's structuralist theorizing differs markedly from that of either Derrida or Foucault, inasmuch as Althusser's reading of Marx utilizes the traditional Marxian "building" metaphor of social formation and aims to give a "scientific" account of ideology that locates ideology in a socio-economic context. Foucault and Derrida, on the other hand, question the "structuralist" assumptions of Marxism, choosing instead to focus on Neitzsche's denunciation of truth, objectivity, and neutrality in knowledge.

What Althusser has contributed to feminist understandings of subjectivity and power is noteworthy, particularly his understanding of *ideology* and how it functions to produce social subjects. For Althusser, ideology is the system of representation by means of which we live in cultures as their products and agents (Althusser, 1971). Ideology transforms biological "materials" into social subjects, obscuring the processes by which the subject is constituted and so enabling the subject to consider this production *natural*. In that "consciousness" is considered self-evident, inevitable, and natural, what consciousness contains is therefore "ideological." Yet, according to Althusser, it is also material in that it is produced by Ideological State Apparatuses (ISAs)—those institutions, rituals, and practices that comprise sociocultural life. Through these ISAs, the subject is "interpellated" to both recognize and misrecognize itself in the institutions and practices that constitute it (Althusser, 1971, p. 163).

An Althusserian analysis of ideology holds that it transforms individuals into subjects by presenting them particular *positions* or "signs of a possible future" that serve the dominant interests in a society (Bourne, 1981, p. 52). This is a significant departure from the analysis of ideology as the imposition of ideas, and a movement toward the analysis of ideology as "discursive practices which prevent anything but an imaginary relation to the real" (Wexler, 1987, pp. 39–40).

Here, of course, is a sticking point for poststructuralists: the notion that language can produce a "false" or imaginary individuality as distinct from a "real" one. For this reason, the notion of interpellation has been subjected in more recent years to much critique and reformulation. However, the primacy Althusser gives to language has continued to be useful in the work of feminist poststructuralists, who have focused on the form through which discourse orders and thereby gives meaning to our world. According to Weedon:

> For feminist poststructuralism, it is language in the form of conflicting discourse which constitutes us as conscious subjects and enables us to give meaning to the world and to act to transform it. (1987, p. 32)

Feminist analyses of patriarchal ideology have been assisted by Althusser's work in moving away from humanist and liberal explanations of what causes social injustice toward an understanding of the importance of the various social structures (systematic sets of relations) unconsciously reproduced by both men and women. While his account of power has been of more use to Marxist feminists than to others, Althusser's understanding of ideology as a systematically integrated and distorting cooperation of linguistic practices, ideals, and values has allowed feminists to move from categorizations of "men as villains" and "women as victims" to a more rigorous examination of social systems and institutional life (Grosz, 1990, p. 71). In focusing on subjectivity as the means by which ideology is reproduced/transformed, Althusser has helped feminists to account for their own sense of identity and how it is related to the variety of social practices in which they are inscribed and in which they act.

For my own research in teacher education, Althusser's notion of the "interpellating" or "hailing" function of ideology continues to be pertinent. It provides a useful conceptual framework for inquiring into the power of neoconservative discourses, born out of the postwelfarism, libertarianism, and determinism of postindustrial capitalism (Sawer, 1982), to "hail" pre-service teachers. The extent to which pre-service teachers beginning their professional preparation are already constituted as the subjects through the power of particular postindustrial discursive orders is important if we are to examine the strengths of the claims of teacher educators and other academics of a "new vocationalism" among undergraduates (Tymitz-Wolf, 1984). This does not mean uncritically accepting the view of avant-garde academics that there is a direct correlation between the triumph of "New Right"[4] discourses and a perceived "hardening" of the pragmatism and "literalness" of student concerns. Nor is it opposed to this understanding. Given Althusser's emphasis on the power of such discourse to be absorbed as natural, and thereby to produce both recognition and misrecognition, my own focus can now be on the effects of interpellation rather than on what it is understood to represent. What I then need to acknowledge is that my own re-presentation of student texts is fictive, texts that are centered through, and limited by, their own internal logic.

It is in grappling with this sort of problem that feminists make use of the poststructuralist deconstructionism of Derrida. Decentering the binary logic of avant-garde text can generate new and more potentially enabling categorizations of pre-service teacher discourse than is evident in modernist texts. It also calls into immediate question the seductively misleading certainty of these newly generated categorizations themselves. This is in keeping with Derrida's concern not with the "truth" of texts but the way a text and its subjects can be constituted and annuled. Derrida describes the decomposition of fixed centers of metaphysics (Wexler, 1987, p. 134), choosing to focus on the means of producing the meanings (always deferred) of various discourses, rather than their "origins" or "social bases." Yet this ought not be understood as simply oppositional to structuralism. Rather, Derrida can be perceived as furthering the work of Saussure and Levi-Strauss in disrupting purely material understandings of ideology, by refusing "a center or a point of presence" that would limit anything but "the free-play of structure" (Derrida, 1970, pp. 247–248). His work has become a critique of structuralism because it stands in opposition to the structuralist view of language as the expression of a prelinguistic primary or fixed essence.

Derrida's deconstruction of texts within the history of philosophy forces the acknowledgment of the oppositions, exclusions, dichotomies, and distinctions that characterize the texts of western metaphysics. His deconstruction is a double procedure, simultaneously occupying a position both within and outside a text. The complex concept of *différance* is his way of playing with a pun to connote simultaneous difference *and* deferral—of the binary oppositional structure of difference/sameness within which it exists and that allows for the use of a text's own system of logic against itself.

Derrida's destabilization of the binary logic of western texts has been important for feminists, particularly in challenging the binary logic of phallocentrism. However, the actual project of extracting a deconstructive method from his work has been very difficult, given the "intertextual" nature of his readings (Grosz, 1990, p. 93). Further, his "apparent intent to defer indefinitely" an encounter of deconstruction with Marxian text has meant that the articulation of a deconstructive politics has not been forthcoming in his own work (Fraser, 1989, p. 69). Nor does he indicate whether it is even possible. *Deconstruction* has since been co-opted to describe a range of processes (from a simple "unpacking" of policy documents and the like, to quite complex intertextual analysis). However, many of these processes have little in common with Derrida's work.

What has been most cautionary for me as a critical teacher educator working with my own and other texts is Derrida's refusal to accept a tradition in critical western scholarship of a center, a "transcendental signifier" that fixes relational symbols in the text from outside the text. My own constant predilection for fixity, foundationalism, or essentialism as a feminist analyzing teacher education texts is constantly challenged, as I come to question the oppositional categories I and others have generated. Teacher education literature, whether avantgarde or not, is plagued with binary formulations (theory/practice, curriculum/pedagogy, college/practicum, student/teacher) and compartmentalization, based as it is on so much of the process/product research literature of the 1970s. Work that provides a "corrective moment" in the unproblematic consumption of these sorts of texts is much needed by the present generation of teacher educators because it unsettles so many preconceptions about truth and falsity. It is for this reason, too, that such work can be and has been so violently resisted.

What are critical teacher educators to make, then, of the power relations of teacher education projects and their own complicity in these relations? For me, the Foucauldian notion that to probe meaning is to probe at one and the same time the social relations of discourse and power is crucial here. Michel Foucault has been most influential in moving contemporary understandings of power away from structuralist attempts to define what power is, and concomitant analyses of the "origins" of power. For Foucault (1980), knowledge and power are inseparable and interrelated, in that there is no power relation without the correlative constitution of a field of knowledge, nor knowledge that does not presuppose and constitute at the same time, power relations (p. 59).

To examine issues of the exercise of power is to examine the processes and struggles of power/knowledge that determine the forms and possible domains of knowledge. Power, then, is not owned by institutions like universities or teachers' colleges, but exists in relationships that are discursively constructed, in that all knowledge is constructed through discourses. It is, therefore, the mutual relationship of constraint and discourse through the functioning of networks of social practices on which his analysis of power is focused (Fraser, 1989, p. 20).

Miller (1990) identifies three important ideas about discourse that Foucault contributes to contemporary analyses of power relations (pp. 115–116). First, discourse is not, and can never be, a transparent "mirror" of the world. Second, the individual subject is a plurality of possible positions and functions, so that the subject is fully described only when the rules of discourse are elaborated. Third, there is no external standard for performing evaluations because value itself is relativized to a particular discourse or set of discourses. While Foucault does allow the potentiality for collective transformation through emancipatory power/knowledge, there is no doubt that he is generally negative about the possibility of individual subjects' being able to take this sort of control over their own lives (Street, 1990, p. 4).

Discourses, for Foucault, are practices, not simply a group of signs, inasmuch as discourses "systematically form the objects of which they speak" (Foucault, 1972, p. 49). In that they embody meaning and social relationships, discourses constitute both subjectivity and power relations. The exercise of power through the effects of discourse is always "a way of acting upon . . . acting subjects by virtue of their acting or being capable of action" (Foucault, 1982, p. 220). This exercise of power incites, induces, seduces, makes easier or more difficult (Foucault, 1982, p. 220). In this sense, discourse as both an instrument and an effect of power can be both the means to prevent an opposing strategy and the means by which an oppositional strategy can begin.

Of crucial importance to teacher education is the idea that discourse is structured by assumptions within which any speaker must operate in order to be heard as meaningful. Because educational sites are centrally involved in the propagation and selective dissemination of discourses, they are sites that can generate both validations of, and exclusions from, the right to speak (Ball, 1990, p. 3). Discourses, once legitimated, can "amplify" or "submerge" the very subjects for whom they are purporting to speak. When university lecturers give mono-logic lectures on the importance of equity in the classroom from their podiums at the front of lecture halls, they engage in practices that may well submerge the identities of "disadvantaged" minorities and others on that same site.

Foucault's understanding of the role played by the various disciplinary discourses through their legitimation of certain forms of power/knowledge also has important ramifications for those who continue to pursue research in ways that fail to challenge how these disciplines constitute the subject as a "governable individual" (Marshall, 1990, p. 26). While Foucault, like Derrida, presents educational researchers with no ready-made "framework" for analyzing power in educational discourse, his work does signal the importance of pursuing analyses of power relations and the importance of maintaining an awareness of the potentially oppressive role of ostensibly liberatory forms of discourse (Lather, 1989; Walkerdine, 1986).

Given women's own histories of marginalization and subjugation, feminists have found that Foucauldian notions of power and resistance confirm many of their own practices, including a refusal of hierarchical organization or representation. Further, Foucault's work appears to confirm the logic of a change of focus from revolution to localized resistance in the form of "strategically located strikes at power's most vulnerable places" (Grosz, 1990, p. 92).

In his understanding of significatory processes as more than playful (unlike Derrida), as formative of the subject, Foucault does indicate a commitment to historical analysis of the *social* (Wexler, 1987, p. 140). His analysis of the nature of discursive practices enables researchers to approach texts as interactive events, instances of the process and product of social meanings in particular discursive contexts. Text and context can be treated as semiotic phenomena, as "modes of meaning" (Halliday & Hasan, 1985, p. 12). Pre-service teachers can be studied as producers of texts. The process of exchange that their texts embody can be articulated as *con*texts. That is, pre-service teachers' articulations of the nature of their work interrogate and are interrogated by the texts of teacher educators, and again in turn interrogate their own texts, in forms of power/knowledge that may enable more than constrain. This does not mean working free from discursive/institutional constraint, but rather that, within these constraints, subjectivities are generated that allow more reflectivity and reflexivity.

BEYOND "FEMINIST" METHOD

Working at the interface of the structuralism of Althusser and the poststructuralisms of Derrida and Foucault, then, means acknowledging two related developments. The first is the reconfiguration of social thought that Rorty (1982) describes as "the rise of text"—a phenomenon that allows poststructuralism to be understood as developing out of, rather than being antithetical to, the structuralist emphasis on language. *Textualism* then may be understood as the culmination of what structuralism and poststructuralism have contributed, both jointly and in opposition, to our understanding of the relation of language with knowledge, power, and subjectivity.

The second development is the role feminists have played in interpreting both structuralist and poststructuralist work on "text" and applying their own interpretations of this work to actual emancipatory projects (e.g., Fraser, 1989; Nicholson, 1990). The extent to which both the imagery and the methodology of textualism have been successfully integrated into the work of feminists "stretching the parameters of postpositivist inquiry" (Lather, 1989, p. 12), provides a different epistemological and theoretical terrain for educational research. The frameworks provided by *feminisms of difference*[5] are not directly structuralist or poststructuralist. They emerge out of constructive engagements with and against the social analytical "textualism" of particular structuralists and poststructuralists (e.g., Fraser, 1989; Grosz, 1990; Harding, 1990; Lather, 1991a).[6] This ought not to be understood as signaling a unified stance among contemporary feminists in response to structuralism, poststructuralism, or the rationality of modernity, nor as a unified and distinctive set of techniques that can be termed "feminist method." Indeed, Harding (1987) argues that any attempt to work toward this would misdirect energies that ought to be devoted to examining the potential strengths of a range of epistemological positions and methodological frameworks. What does seem to unify feminist concerns, however, is the challenge of "changing the territory where knowledge is located" (Tomm, 1989, p. 10) for the purpose of translating interventions with liberatory intent into actual practices. So feminists continue to explore the question of which theoretical tack best serves contemporary women's interests (Di Stephano, 1990, p. 66). The untidiness of many contemporary studies reflects the necessary uncertainty (and difficulty) of this straddling of agendas. Nevertheless, this untidiness is appropriate in educational research where problems are not solved by a new formula or scientific breakthrough. Di Stephano (1990) speaks of such contemporary strategies as "inhabiting a constantly shifting ground of emerging and dissolving differences" (p. 68)—theoretically appealing yet complex and unnerving.

The fact that feminist *postrationalist* social analyses go beyond a disciplinary realignment to challenge the very philosophical foundations of objectivism is indicative of a new mood in academic theorizing that is highly resistant to categorization. This has meant, at least in part, transcending not only the "structure-agency" or "individual-society" binaries that have impeded radical analyses of historical movements of class cultural action. It also involves refusing the binary logic of research methodology that understands subjectivity or "reflexivity" of the type embodied in the so-called thick descriptions of ethnography (Geertz, 1973) as *the* alternative to positivism (Wexler, 1987, p. 43). As with the relation between poststructuralism and its predecessor, postrationalism does not reject out of hand the methodologies of positivism, but moves beyond the boundaries positivism set itself for producing and articulating knowledge. For feminist postpositivists, achieving this movement has necessitated the development of *internal* critiques for analyzing issues of subjectivity and power (Grosz, 1990).

This is important to the researcher/pedagogue for several reasons. First, it allows understanding of one's own consciousness and that of the other participants as in a constant state of production and reproduction rather than as a source of ideas. Second, it enables analysis that is open, "unresolved," and more flexible in its ability to respond to textual "fragments," seeking not to tidy language but to generate inquiry in which fragmentation and contradiction are the very stuff of analysis. Third, feminist poststructuralist analyses provide a means for pre-service teachers to probe the partiality, openness, and contingency of their own texts about teaching, to the extent that they can be assisted in working out of these frameworks.

In asserting that "the personal is political" more than a decade before Henriques and associates' critique, "second-wave" feminism had already signaled its rejection of an individual/society dualism. Yet the more feminists focused on the public/private split, the more they were to note the silence of the literature of modernity about the private sphere, so important to the social constitution of women as subjects (Wolff, 1985, p. 43). As a consequence, contemporary feminist theorists have taken up the challenge of moving beyond mere antisexist critiques to construct "new paradigms and models, methods and norms for knowledge" (Gunew, 1990, p. 3). This has entailed engaging with notions of power and subjectivity as the *objects* of feminist scrutiny, rather than regarding them as overarching frameworks or criteria for *judging* feminist theory (Grosz, 1990, p. 109).

Some implications for teacher education may be that, instead of giving another evangelical lecture on "the importance of being feminist," critical teacher educators might do better to subject a range of pedagogical processes to analysis that is informed by feminist theorizing. In this way a "dollop" of feminist theory can be appropriately reworked into a set of useful practices for engaging with actual strategies for teaching and learning. I am not arguing for an end to feminists' giving lectures about feminism, or discrete topics on gender. However, it seems to me that the "rent-a-feminist" mentality that leaves it to the woman in cheesecloth to give what to the students can seem to be the predictable feminists' lament makes it too easy to substitute a token gesture for real on-going engagement. In this way, teacher education undergraduates can and do bypass the challenge of attending to the social injustices that remain unresolved in classrooms at all educational levels.

Instead, feminisms as processes can be woven into the fabric of our daily work in ways that allow them to be both explicit and implicit in our institutional practices. As a coordinator of core subjects involving over 700 students, I felt it was more valuable to make the seminar enrollment explicitly an equity issue than to give a monolithic and "quick-fix" lecture on equity. This meant that caregivers and others who could demonstrate need for special consideration would be observed by other students to enroll first. Not only did this circumvent the "survival of the fittest" scramble for the most desirable tutorial time slots, but it allowed this group of pre-service teachers an early opportunity to critique and consider the implications of this sort of positive discrimination for their own future practice. The "how to" of resistance was from this time on a perennial theme for debates about pedagogy and for pedagogical processes in the newly formed groups.

The issue of whether certain postmodern challenges to these debates can be co-opted for the purposes of resistance, or whether they are, in Irigaray's (1985) terms, the "last ruse" of patriarchy remains unresolved for many feminist teachers. While contemporary feminisms exist in a state of tension with Enlightenment assumptions, they also exist in a state of tension with those for whom the Enlightenment project is wholly abandoned. In that feminisms "grew out of the cracks and silences in the old radical articulations" (Hebdidge, 1988, p. 188), their critiques of totalizing Enlightenment narratives have historical continuity, with postmodernity simply providing another source of such critical ideas. Disparate theories of power and subjectivity have therefore been put to work against each other (Grosz, 1990, p. 111) in the service of the affirmation of difference. Thus feminist science guards against any postmodern notion of "a happy polytheism of language games" that lapses into a-politicism, as Benhabib indicates:

> [T]here are times when philosophy cannot afford to be a "gay science", for reality itself becomes deadly serious. To deny that the play of language games may not turn into a matter of life and death and that the intellectual cannot remain the priest of many gods but must take a stance is cynical. (1990, p. 123)

Contemporary feminists' concern in maintaining a resistant agenda has meant countering allegiance to the historical norm of objectivity as well as remaining skeptical about the value of postmodernism for women (Di Stephano, 1990). This may be interpreted, unfairly, as ambivalence, or as wanting "a dollar each way." The strength of such a view is that it opens up new possibilities because of its recognition of "the permanent partiality of the feminist point of view" (Harding, cited in Di Stephano, 1990, p. 75). This has assisted educators in general to pursue less repressive critical pedagogy, emphasizing enabling work with research participants (Ellsworth, 1989; Gore, 1991; Lather, 1986; Lesko, 1988; Noffke, 1991; Orner & Brennan, 1989; Westcott, 1979; Yates, 1990). Such researchers have made the focus of their work *praxis*—the dialectical tension between and the interactive reciprocal shaping of theory and practice (Lather, 1986, p. 258).

For such feminists, the poststructural emphasis on language and the deconstruction of subjectivity is most appropriate to this focus (Davies, 1987; Grosz, 1990; Irigaray, 1984). The privileging of *discourse*, of partial narratives about the world over whole narratives, allows exploration of the intimate relationship between knowledge and interest, the latter being understood as "a 'standpoint' from which to grasp reality" (Haraway, cited in Ellsworth, 1989, p. 304). This has meant grappling with a problematic residual commitment to Marxian tendencies and frames of reference (Hebdidge, 1988, p. 192). It is to Gramsci that many feminist writers have turned for less monolithic, more engaging emancipatory discourse, and to Foucault for a constant and corrective reminder that every creed is potentially oppressive.

In the research models born out of such theorizing, the unidimensional clarity of the view of educational researcher as expert, detached observer of the activities of insiders is replaced by fragmenting, multiple images, a play of surfaces among elements. These models also attend to specific problems in local conditions. They must therefore be open to the sort of discrepant data produced by idiosyncratic circumstances and by a reflexive approach on the part of both researcher and researched (Elliot, 1988). The research process becomes "a form of border crossing" (Giroux, 1991, p. 51), a deliberate transgression against traditional territorial boundaries in teacher education for the purposes of making visible "the historically and socially constructed strengths and limitations of those places and borders we inherit which frame our discourses and social relations" (Giroux, 1991, p. 52).

The problem with exhortations such as that provided from Giroux, is that there seems to be so little here to guide what one might actually do. All practitioners, including teachers and teacher educators, understandably become impatient with texts that operate at a level of generality that gives the appearance of deliberately avoiding contact with daily practices. Again, it is as though the mire of technique must be shunned in order to avoid the sin of technocratic rationality. And again it is feminists who have insisted on asking and telling what this might actually mean in terms of doing educational research.

RESEARCH AND PEDAGOGY: MAKING NEW SENSE

One way to reclaim our daily practices as valid sites of inquiry is to refuse the binary formulation of our teacher education work as either research or pedagogy. Of course, there will always be aspects of our work, e.g., publication, that may be quite clearly located in one domain or the other; however, there are potential rewards for our students in our refusing this binary in terms of the quality of our interventions into their pedagogical practices. *Research-as-pedagogy* is not a conflation of teaching and research because it is not an escape from rigor nor from the sites on which we engage. On the contrary, coming down from the knee of God involves "working in anti-foundational ways to break with the signs that encode valid inquiry" (Lather, 1993, p. 2). More than fleeting attention must therefore be paid to the epistemological, evidentiary, political-ethical, or operational issues raised by teacher education-as-research. What assumes great importance is the way these issues are related. Understanding research as a particular sort of strategic intervention allows a greater focus on the relational aspects of educational inquiry. Grosz's understanding of strategy is useful here:

> Strategy involves recognising the situation and alignments of power within and against which it operates. It needs to know its adversary intimately in order to strike at its most vulnerable points. It must also seek certain (provisional) goals and future possibilities with which it may replace prevailing norms and ideals, demonstrating that they are not the only possibilities. They *can* be superseded. (1990, p. 59)

Any intervention that is informed by this sort of imperative embarks on research that eschews both research "objectivism" and the potential for passive noninterventionism in interpretive ethnography (Gitlin, Siegel, & Boru, 1988). While guarding against the tendency for certain sorts of interpretive work to slide into subjectivism, *research-as-pedagogy* is nevertheless in keeping with the broad "interpretive turn" (Rabinow & Sullivan, 1979) in the social sciences, a trend away from "grand theorizing" and toward a reinvigorated interest in hermeneutics and the production of open-ended, dialogic work.

As with psychology, neither hermeneutics nor dialectics ought to be understood as monolithic in terms of definition or contribution to scientific inquiry. While hermeneutics is generally understood as roughly synonymous with the art of interpretation, particularly in association with the humanities, it has also been understood as identifying a general philosophical method, a science of linguistic understanding, a phenomenology of existence, and specific systems of interpretation of myths and symbols (Bartlett, 1990, p. 8). Dialectics, on the other hand, is more closely associated with critical theory in and for social scientific analysis, again embodying a range of analytical tools and methodologies. What hermeneutics and dialectics bring into combination is apparently contrary emphases—a historical tradition of wholeness, interpretation, and meaning, and a critical tradition of contradiction, change, and transcendence (Bartlett, 1990, p. 10).

An important aspect of the "interpretive turn" in research, informed out of this combination of traditions of thought, is the new understanding it brings to the crucial role played by the researcher as a "truth tester." If the researcher's version of the truth is to be accepted as scholarly and worthy, the assumptions and beliefs that underpin the way researcher-researched relations as "outsider-insider" relations must be attended to. Indeed, how these assumptions are framed in the research is an absolutely fundamental component of the work of the researcher (Elliot, 1988). For Gadamer, the implication is not that the researcher suspends bias, for the growth of understanding is not about freedom from bias but its reconstruction. Indeed it is the realization that "all understanding inevitably involves some prejudice" that gives the hermeneutical problem its primary thrust (Gadamer, 1975, p. 239). The researcher's reconstruction must be able to include the "truth" of all of the participants whose observations, interpretations, and judgments ought to inform the research. Methodology must allow the discrepant data of outsiders "as insiders" (Elliot, 1988, p. 164). This is an imperative that educational research has been slow to acknowledge (Gottlieb, 1989, p. 131), despite the work done "after the new sociology" (Wexler, 1987).

The approach I take to research-as-pedagogy is informed out of a "new contextualism" in which knowing is a historical and cultural practice, and where research methods are historically and culturally produced tools for the production of knowledge (Wexler, 1987, p. 84). Such inquiry leaves no doubt about the researcher's own prejudgment, committed as it is to the development of an enabling and interactive approach to knowledge building that is theoretically and methodologically provocative (Lather, 1986, p. 260). Provocativeness is essential if the research model is to respond to calls for eliminating the dichotomy between educational research and the construction of emancipatory theory, and between emancipatory theory and "factory floor" practices (Yates, 1990). It means signaling overtly its own political character, by working *within/against* the "legitimate" discourses of positivist research methodology as well as its own radical feminist social critique (Lather, 1991a). Patti Lather's work in examining what it means to do valid research deserves greater elaboration here.

In *Research as Praxis* (1986), Lather followed the call of Reason and Rowan (1981, p. xiii) to expand traditional concepts of validity toward "an objectively subjective" inquiry. While she noted the ongoing need for *triangulation* to allow counterpatterns to emerge and *construct* validity, in that research must operate in a conscious context of theory building, Lather argued that two further issues are vital to a project committed to social justice: *face* validity and *catalytic* validity (1986, pp. 271–272). For Lather, face validity occurs when emergent analysis is recycled through at least a subsample of respondents to establish the "trustworthiness" of data. At the same time, she acknowledges the problem illuminated by Gramscian understandings of hegemony, that subjects may accept the very conclusions that disallow action in their own best interests. The notion of "catalytic validity" is descriptive of the degree to which the research participants are refocused and ener-

gized toward new ways of knowing in order to engage more power-
fully in their own practice.

In Lather's more recent work, issues around "the politics of knowing and being known" (Lather, 1991b) in educational inquiry have been
probed further by using the postmodern ferment to interrogate critical
scholarship. This interrogation has helped feminists to acknowledge,
by means of a "doubled movement of inscription and subversion," the
ways that feminism is both outside and yet inscribed within western
logocentrism, patriarchal rationality and imperialistic practices
(Lather, 1989, p. 7). Lather notes the profound linguistic turn in social
theory exemplified by Derrida's work, focusing less on truth and more
on the production of "truth effects" (Lather, 1991a, p. 31). Her concep-
tion of a postpositivist research methodology as working within/
against the complexity, contingency, and fragility of its own discursive
practices is an example of this.

Lather argues for refusal of recuperation and great transformation
by feminists and other social critics in favor of "foster[ing] differences
and let[ting] contradictions remain in tension" (Lather, 1993, p. 13).
She reworks the notion of validity in ways that are subversive of all
forms of orthodoxy, drawing on a range of poststructuralist writers
in generating antifoundational framings for "transgressive" research
(1993, p. 8). Among her many "reinscriptions," the term "rhizomatic
validity" (Lather, 1993, p. 14) is used to describe that research rigor
which dissolves interpretations and interrupts impetuous quests to
grasp at understanding, in favor of maintaining a process of meticulous and patient documentary. Lather argues (1993, p. 14) that functioning rhizomatically is acting via relay, a circuitous journey among
intersections, nodes, regionalizations, and multi-centered complexities. This metaphor denotes a departure from the notion of linear progression from a fixed point.

For teacher educators/researchers, the implications of these intentions are many. They include acknowledging the importance of valid
and rigorous inquiry while at the same time seeking to reconceptualize
what this might mean for the relationship of research and pedagogy.
So little is surety; so much is skepticism. The contributions of neo-
feminists like Lather to understanding possibilities for current educational research evoke more disquiet from traditional researchers than
"predictable" reiterations of feminism as "antiscience." This has never
really threatened the hegemonic status of positivism, and certainly not
in teacher education.

Research that refuses Shakespeare's dictum by "altering when it
alteration finds" is, of course, much more challenging to engage in

than research that works with the logic of the shoehorn. Straddling modernist and postmodernist agendas does require the researcher to explain the unsettling of assumptions in order to provide corrective reflexive moments throughout a study. The metaphor I have used elsewhere for engagement in modernist/postmodernist educational practices is that of constantly trying to adjust a sheet that is a size too small in order to ensure that no vulgar part of one's ideological anatomy is left out in the cold for very long (McWilliam, 1993b). Yet it is this very inability to be comfortable in old discursive orders that will allow the rethinking necessary to the condition of "postmodern" education (Kiziltan, Bain, & Canizares, 1990).

Avant-garde educational discourse has not escaped the tendency of other types of legitimate educational discourse to privilege its own expert versions of the truth in educational matters (Tripp, 1990, p. 71), an issue I take up more fully in the next chapter. This invalidates the claims of those whose voices have broken the rules "by grounding their knowledge in immediate emotional, social and psychic experiences of oppression" (Ellsworth, 1989, p. 305). Further, in their very lack of interest in self-examination (Weber, 1986; Zeichner & Tabachnick, 1981), teacher educator researchers in the past, whether driven by "emancipatory" intent or not, have failed to acknowledge the limits imposed on the student voice through the relations of their own research acts as well as their daily pedagogical practices at the pre-service level.

Pre-service teachers typically experience a "double-dose" of powerlessness since they continue to experience the state of being a student while at the same time they are introduced to the sort of oppression that is experienced by the least powerful of teachers. The practicum (prac) experience is therefore a crucial moment in their training. It is here that students-as-teachers are confronted by what they perceive as their own inadequacy—their lack of pedagogical experience-as-knowhow. The post-prac stories through which new identities are constructed so often concede almost everything to factory floor or "hands-on" teaching experience. (The pervasiveness of this "manual" metaphor in pre-service teacher texts is analyzed in Chapter 4.) This reconstruction so often situates pre-service teachers as the most ignorant of teachers, in spite of the possibility that they may be more cognizant of innovative strategies and contemporary policy than many experienced teachers.

The object of inquiry, however, must not be understood as letting anyone "off the hook" of engagement at the level of critique—researcher or researched—inasmuch as it continues to focus on resisting oppressive ways of knowing and being known (Ellsworth, 1989, p.

322). Authoritarian research relations should not be replaced by research that installs a "successor regime" (Harding, 1986) of patronage. Elevating the "partial narratives" of the researched to the status of a totalizing narrative—"the truth" about pre-service needs—will hardly be an appropriate development. Such a course leaves open the strong possibility that a sort of flabby romantic talk about "meeting individual needs" and "developing full potential" replaces rigorous self-critique. "I'm OK, You're OK" is a ready substitute for "How do I say, Whom do I say?"

DISPLAYING RESEARCH DIFFERENTLY

One example of many dilemmas raised by working both inside and outside the structural logic of our own texts is the form in which the research is to be presented. In educational report writing, for example, the notion still prevails that theory, method, and results are to be written as discrete chapters "in tandem," carriages on the research train headed away from fragmentation and toward unity, from doubt and toward certainty. There is a great potential for "leaving theory behind" in this linear articulation of the theory/method/results nexus, in that it fails to signal the embeddedness of theory in the entire research task, or to make evident the extent to which the research ought to be generative of theory rather than merely report "objective findings." To depict theory as a tidy point of embarkation and "results-as-findings" as a convenient point of disembarkation will nevertheless misconstrue the reflexive nature of the research project and the epistemological assumptions within which it locates itself.

Lather's (1989) strategy of "turning text into display and interaction among perspectives" and "presenting material rich enough to bear re-analysis in different ways" (p. 15) is one that attempts to rework academic research as texts. She seeks to bring the reader into the analysis by "a dispersive impulse which fragments univocal authority" and thereby interrupts social relations of dominance (p. 15). The research task is reconceptualized as the production of textuality in a form of narrative, "a point of intersection between two subjectivities" that could easily have produced a different narrative with different emphases in different conditions (p. 17). She cites a range of feminist studies, including her own, as examples of research that is committed to "less oppressive ways of knowing" (pp. 18–25).

To approach the writing of research inquiry this way is to tell stories that end neither in a fixed body of comprehended knowledge nor in overcoming textual ambiguity. It is to work toward "a new understanding of confusion" in this sense, but this is preferable to the "confusion of understanding" that has been belied by the apparent clarity of positivism's incursions into the realm of making meaning. In disallowing claims to certainty and to totalizing narratives, this type of methodology declares its awareness of the inescapable relationship between power, text, and belief.

Many studies have been conducted that utilize empirical *or* discourse-analytical *or* interactive methods in education. It is not that such studies cannot tell us more about the nature of educational knowledge and practice, but that in many cases their implications "wither on the vine" for the very inability of the research methodology, conceived of as necessarily a singular entity, to push on to productive outcomes for all. What has been made possible in a new postrationalist atmosphere of uncertainty and critique is not an end to producing valid, rigorous inquiry that opens itself to public scrutiny, but experimentation with research forms and processes, and the sort of theorizing out of which they might be informed. My initial (and appropriate) trepidation about wading into the murky waters of experimentation with theory/method by working within/against critical pedagogy has been replaced by a cautious optimism about the rewards such an endeavor can have for all educational work. The challenge for teacher educators becomes the development of means of inquiry that "denaturalize" the many shifting relations of power in our daily pedagogical work rather than disguising and/or sustaining them. Such collaborative processes are long overdue in teacher education research, given its lamentable history of social relations between researchers and preservice teachers. It is time to tell different tales to make a difference.

CHAPTER 3

QUICK AND DULL

The Folkloric Discourses of Teacher Education

TEACHER EDUCATION FOLKLORE

My thesaurus locates "folklore" in two related linguistic sites. The term appears in the context of "maturity and ripeness" as well as "decline and decay." It is appropriate to apply this term when discussing teacher education debates, since teacher education discourses are in a symbiotic state of both maturation and decay, the overripe fruits of a great deal of educational labor. While still palatable to many, they now lack the crisp texture or bite of the "forbidden fruit" of transgressive methodologies and pedagogies being produced out of postrationalist theorizing.[1]

This tale is about changing the nature of the struggles in which I have been involved to articulate the needs of pre-service teachers. I became increasingly aware of these struggles as I became embroiled in the micropolitics of teacher education conferences and forums. Disagreements were also manifested in academic writing about teacher education and interactions with colleagues in my own and similar institutions. While I noted vast differences of opinion, I began to feel as a new teacher educator that a number of propositions had congealed into truisms that shaped and limited debates about the relevance of particular types of teacher training programs. The fact that there seemed to be so little disagreement over some very fundamental issues and such clear lines of demarcation over others left me wondering about the certainty and the pervasiveness of much of this talk. Could the needs of pre-service teachers really be so predictable, given the diversity of personal life histories and the uncertainty about future clientele and work places? The story told below attempts to provide some map of the terrain on which my own versions of *relevant* teacher education have been constructed. Its aim is to disrupt old contestations in order to reconstruct critical debate about relevance.

TALKING RELEVANCE: OLD LORE FOR TEACHER EDUCATION FOLK

Probably the most pervasive and instantly recognizable feature of the vocabularies practicing teachers use in framing talk about their work is the language of the psy-disciplines, in particular educational psychology. This language has historically provided the vocabularies for orthodox research in teacher education as well as setting the parameters of "valid" methodology for inquiry into matters affecting preservice teachers. The phenomenon has been part of a broader tendency to treat educational research in general as "a species of educational psychology" (Eisner, 1983, p. 14). The difficulty with the dominance of psychology is not that psychology itself has been necessarily a monolithic force of oppression and distortion. Instead, as I pointed out in the previous chapter, the notions of individuality produced by discourses of social regulation to which psychology has contributed have failed to address issues of subjectivity. This has prevented examination of the ways in which pre-service teachers reconstruct their own selves through languages that are regulated by particular sets of social and power relations.

Critics of teacher socialization literature have noted, for example, the relationship that exists between the excessive psychologizing of the term *socialization* itself and the paucity of its powers of explanation in conveying the richness and diversity of the social relations of preservice preparation (Battersby & Ramsay, 1983). Complex and on-going processes have been studied as static phenomena, a "pre-given universe of objects" rather than one "produced by the active doings of subjects" (Giddens, 1976, p. 160). In extolling the virtues of the conceptual clarity and methodological "purity" of such objectivism, at the expense of innovation and social vitality, researchers have been and still are producing a historically encapsulated view of research. There has been little understanding of such inquiry as a historical and contextual practice (Wexler, 1987, p. 82).

New ways of theorizing teacher work that are emerging in preservice teacher research make it clear that mainstream inquiry, while predominantly behaviorist, has not simply been bound by determinism. It has continued, like the objects of its inquiry, both to shape and to be shaped by its own development and by social developments external to it (Yates, 1990, p. 17). Yet despite shifts to ethnographic and action research in the 1980s, it was the "clear images" of positivist work, in particular behaviorist and "attitudinal" studies of pre-service experiences, that framed the relevance debate in teacher education policy documents and course reviews in the 1980s (Battersby & Retallick, 1988). And it was the clear images of definitive studies, continually recycled in the discursive practices of teacher educators/researchers, that informed folklore for articulating "student teacher needs." The quest for cause-effect, for predicability, for certitude in psychostatistical research, ensured that "findings" were easily incorporated into the definitive stories told about pre-service experience.

Stories about the relevance of practices, conceived of as content or process, were generally informed by appeals to proven truths or definitive data obtained by one-shot or pre- and postsurveys (Battersby & Ramsay, 1983, p. 80). Tisher and Wideen's (1990) analysis of teacher education research trends to 1990 shows that there were few if any dramatic advances in the way the process of teacher education was being conceptualized despite the plethora of studies conducted. Within this positivist research culture, many teacher educators/researchers have been hard at work examining the issue of the relevance of their courses in meeting the needs of student teachers, however defined, and in defending their own contributions to this task. The energy devoted to probing captive populations of students has been, and still is, quite remarkable by any standards. Indeed, I would be surprised if there is any "attitudinal" or other dimension of student teachers' lives that has escaped quantification.

Constantly recycled within teacher education discourse itself, these research "findings" have allowed certain propositions to become so far beyond dispute that they could go without saying. The proposition that "self-and-survival" was the driving logic of pre-service teacher talk about needs, for example, solidified into time-honored "truth" about pre-service teachers, legitimating its status as *folklore*. Despite studies contradicting Fuller's (1969) oft-quoted analysis of a "proven" developmental sequence of concerns around "self" and "survival" (e.g., Maxie, 1989), this proposition became part of a system of rules for talking and writing about pre-service teacher needs.

Submitting this talking and writing to scrutiny helps educators to understand how our educational "dialects" resist, accommodate, and inform systems of rules for articulating relevance in teacher education programs and debates. The effects of the discursive system in which talk is generated about the needs of pre-service teachers can be understood as constituting a "regime of truth" in which discourses about teacher education compete for legitimacy. Foucault says:

Each society has its regime of truth, its "general politics" of truth; that is, the types of discourse which it accepts and makes function as true; the mechanisms and instances which enable one to distinguish true and false statements, the means by which each is sanctioned; the techniques and procedures accorded value in the acquisition of truth; the status of those who are charged with saying what counts as true. (1980, p. 131)

Framed by this regime of truth, debates have raged about the relevance or otherwise of initial teacher education practices. A whole network of taken-for-granted propositions has informed these debates. These assumptions include:

- Students will always differentiate between "theory" and "practice" and eschew the former.
- The more "practice" the better (quantity and quality being usually held to be synonymous when considering the role of the field experience).
- School culture is in opposition to and wins out over university culture in the "battle for hearts and minds" of pre-service teachers.
- Pre-service teachers enter idealistic or "soft" and leave realistic or "hardened," an attitudinal change in which the main ingredient is the practicum experience.
- Pre-service teachers are ideologically conservative, and therefore fail to comprehend the political nature of the teaching act.
- Pre-service teachers are less competent/skilled than they used to be (this is a perennial of conservative policy discourse about teacher education in the 1980s and 1990s).

These folkloric assumptions are manifest in a range of discursive sites: staff meetings within particular schools, territorial struggles in reviews of teacher education programs conducted within universities, external policy documents and reviews of teacher education. They are sometimes couched as anecdotal and perceived evidence or standard student complaints, not "wrong" as much as simplistic. Meanwhile teacher educators continue to bemoan an apparent lack, however defined, in their charges, some fretting over perceived deficits in student teachers—their suitability for recruitment, mastery of curriculum disciplines, and the like, and others fretting over a perceived mindless pragmatism in the student response to "emancipatory" agendas.

According to teacher educators who see teacher education as a critical/political project, the regime of truth within teacher education has the effect of rendering critical pedagogy "impractical," inasmuch as it is not driven by the occupational attributes of "life in schools" (Smith & Zantiotis, 1988b, p. 2). While critical writers argue the very "impractical" consequences of such a vision of practicality for those entering the profession, an unfortunate and indirect effect has been to blame the victim. The "problem" with pre-service teachers is their failure to transcend this logic in favor of a socially critical version of educational reality. In this version of pre-service teacher needs, undergraduates are either aggressively and knowingly subverting a critical agenda, or naively opting for an apprenticeship of immersion at the expense of the empowering critique of the nature of teacher work. Either way, they are ripe for reconstructing.

There are, of course, teacher educators who do not identify with academic scholarship at all, let alone critical scholarship. This position may have some merit, particularly where teachers are poorly served by the work of academics. The problem with this stance is that this can quickly slide into a sort of idiosyncratic anti-intellectual populism that is unhelpful for the fact that it allows the relevance debate to stagnate or cease altogether.

RELEVANCE: DETERMINISM VERSUS CRITICAL PEDAGOGY

It is high time that we move beyond "treat[ing] the symptoms and leav[ing] the disease untouched" (Ellsworth, 1989, p. 306). This means reopening and reexamining the "relevance" debate at the level of the discursive structures in which it has come to be articulated. The task for researchers is not to find new data that can "disprove" the time-honored "findings" of research on or about pre-service teachers. Given that new understandings come from new metaphors, the project involves generating a richer metaphorical language than traditional teacher education talk, whose truisms have been well and truly milked of what they offer.

Meanwhile, outside academe, the relevance debate in teacher education reviews and policy initiatives is still played out within an instrumentalist orientation, unchallenged by counterhegemonic studies that might draw attention to asymmetrical relations of power within or outside educational institutions (Battersby & Retallick, 1988). This is not simply a refusal on the part of policy makers to grapple with the complexities of educating teachers for postmodern times, but is a manifestation, at least to some degree, of a gradual decline in the academic interest shown in teacher socialization itself (Atkinson & Delamont, 1985, p. 307). Despite a plethora of teacher education research projects in the 1980s, the relevance debate has become worn out and trivialized because of the limitations of past work that was theoretically and methodologically simplistic, often mere mimicry of what are understood to be scientific procedures (Bannister, 1981; Diamond, 1988). Moreover, attention has been drawn to the fact that more "progressive" teacher education research, which huddles under the qualitative umbrella, cannot always be identifiable theoretically as anything more than "nonquantitative" (Bartlett, 1989). Overall, the dominance of inventory/questionnaire perspectives on skills, attitudes and beliefs rather than exploration of students as generators of meaning means a weak and ambiguous knowledge base, still articulated as "theory/ practice" (Zeichner, 1986, p. 27).

The dominance of deterministic research has been held responsible not only for the absence of substantial debate about teacher education but also, and as a consequence, the failure of educational reform to restructure the processes of teacher education at the micro-level. Reform has been understood as either a technical or, in the case of interpretive inquiry, a practical task rather than as participatory and collaborative (Carr & Kemmis, 1986, pp. 156–157), a product of the relations of the research act itself. The concerns of Popkewitz more than a decade ago have therefore remained the concerns of many teacher educators who have distanced themselves from behaviorist models:

> The technical definitions of educational problems and the procedural responses to reform in teacher education are legitimated by much of the research in the field. Most research tends to view teaching as a form of human engineering and teacher education as the most efficient way to provide new recruits with the specific behaviours and attitudes of the people who practise teaching . . . what is ignored are the ways in which teacher education imposes . . . patterns of work and thought. (1979, pp. 1–3)

Deterministic modes of inquiry in teacher education fail entirely to perceive or acknowledge the talk in which they are embedded. Analyses of versions of relevance as sets of socially constructed speaking practices that are constantly open to change is beyond the parameters of mainstream research method.

Feminist poststructuralists will not resolve the issues for teacher educators, nor should they, because the debates must continue. However, poststructuralist theory can revitalize debate by highlighting the fact that relevance texts produced by stakeholders in the teacher education project are constituted out of particular positions of power available to the participants in institutionally produced sets of meanings. So the speaking and writing of teacher educators and pre-service teachers can be understood differently. No longer are these texts things or even sets of ideas but languages that "speak" academics and students as subjects. Moreover, it is possible to understand the knowledge of both researcher and researched as framed within a particular system of speech rules yet open to challenge and change.

This understanding is a departure from the notion that the material reproduction of society results from practices that are articulated through a single logic. It situates the problem of talking and writing itself—of the constitution of new subjects and the transformation of these subjects—within the realm of *discourse*. Discourse, as conceptualized here, is a departure from the classical structuralist notion[2] of language in that it brings into focus the social-historical conditions under which words change their meaning (Thompson, 1984, p. 234). According to Pecheux (1975), we articulate "meanings" through expressions that are already constituted by particular "discursive formations." These discursive formations are in turn constituted out of particular social formations, although this is not to be conflated with a Marxist understanding of fixed class relations. The realm of discourse is a realm of relationships, one that is constantly changing. Laclau elaborates on this dynamic:

> Discursive articulation among . . . different levels [of society] constitutes the unity of the social agent. This linking of different positionalities occurs through discourse. This unity can . . . be disarticulated and recomposed by other discourses. In this sense, the subjectivity of social agents as such is constantly changing because it's not a homogeneous subjectivity but a constantly recreated unity depending on a whole relation of forces in society at a given moment. (Laclau & Mouffe, 1982, p. 100)

What is important here is the temporary and open nature of the discursive alliances forged at the micro-political level, including those characteristic of the organization of teacher education institutions. To accept this is to challenge the idea that talk in teacher education is only "theoretical" or "practical," a problem that has bedeviled teacher education since its inception (Hogan, 1988; Smyth, 1987). Acceptance of Laclau's argument also challenges the notion of an inevitable progression that is played out between the time that students enter and the time they leave teacher education institutions: idealism to realism, humanism to custodialism, etc. (Feldman, 1972; Hoy, 1969; Lacey, 1977; Lauglo, 1975; Maynard, 1975). Indeed, it is to challenge the very folklore that has become the common sense of teacher socialization. This "invented" knowledge disallows contradictory versions of the way students give meaning to their own professional preparation. Knowledge about students congeals into folklore—a system of binaries for writing about pre-service teachers that has developed out of the practice of "studying down" on them.

These binary formulations are constructed in a range of studies. For example, in noting changes in pre-service teacher "attitudes" over time, a continuum of idealism (humanism) to realism (custodialism) has been invented to describe and explain change (e.g., Deal & Chatman, 1989; Hoy & Rees, 1977; Lacey, 1977; Lauglo, 1975; Maxie, 1989; Maynard, 1975; Palonsky & Jacobson, 1989). In a related group of studies, course-effectiveness perceptions and attitudes toward particular features of college programs have been written as theory/practice distinctions (e.g., Borthwick, 1986; Carr, 1980; Fuller, 1969; Goodman, 1986; Goodman & Alder, 1985; Joyce, 1978; Lemlech & Kaplan, 1990; Paine, 1990; Taylor, 1975). Changing recruitment patterns, selection, and composition of the student body are still addressed through a binary which distinguishes the mainstream (white middle class) from Others (e.g., Howey & Gardner, 1983; Hukill & Hughes, 1983; Newton & Brathwaite, 1987). Finally, the influence of the practicum on pre-service teachers is addressed as "real world" schooling as opposed to the university cloister (e.g., Applegate, 1987; Armaline & Hoover, 1989; Sellars, 1988; Williams, 1989).

Critical/political teacher education literature has not been immune to this. As a teacher educator, I have identified my own work as located in critical debates about teacher preparation informed by a range of social-reconstructionist literature that has been termed the avant-garde scholarship of the 1980s (Smith & Zantiotis, 1988a). In this sort of writing, academics identified and debated (usually within the ranks of the "converted") the problems of teacher education as a cultural and discursive system. Avant-garde analyses drew on the theoretical framework provided by the new sociology of the 1970s and subsequent socially critical work. For more than a decade after Young's seminal work, *Knowledge and Control* (1971), elaborations on the theme of the inherently political nature of teacher work proliferated. Analyses were informed by a range of perspectives: neo-Marxist and other politically oriented scholarship, feminism, psychoanalysis, a revitalized hermeneutics and phenomenology, structuralism, poststructuralism, and historical discussions of the field of curriculum (Shaker & Kridel, 1989).

In broad terms, the literature identified many of the problems of teacher education as springing from an instrumentalist tradition of teacher education that separated means from ends, research from practice, knowing from doing (Munby & Russell, 1989, p. 72). Behaviorism and essentialism were the bogeys. The dominance of behaviorism in driving an essentialist teacher education curriculum, particularly through the process-product research of the 1970s, was held responsible for simplistic understandings of the nature of teacher work and, hence, inappropriate programs of teacher preparation.

In the 1980s, pressure was increasingly applied to augment, to challenge, and to contextualize traditional ways of understanding how teachers come to perceive their work, and the implications of this for initial teacher education. Zeichner (1986) argued that neither evolutionary explanations nor psychoanalytic studies successfully linked perspectives of individuals to forms of meaning and rationality that dominate social life. Further, inquiry that focuses on the influence of formal programs of learning (Hodges, 1982; Katz & Raths, 1982) or field experiences (Williams, 1989) has not illuminated the social mechanisms operating over the duration of these activities.

Calls for cogent and less dismissive analyses of the role of pre-service preparation have moved some teacher educators to reconceptualize teacher work, and the role played by pre-service preparation in constituting it. A growing body of literature has addressed a perennial neglect of context by bringing forward for scrutiny teacher education's "hidden curriculum." Lortie's (1975) concept of an "apprenticeship of observation," Dale's (1977) critique of the "liberal individualistic" cognitive style of British teacher education courses, Popkewitz's (1985, 1987) exposure of the value-laden covert processes of teacher education, Connell's (1985) evidence of the psychologization of pre-service teachers, Denscombe's (1982, 1985) analysis of the "hidden pedagogy" of pre-service programs, Hatton's (1989, 1991) studies of teachers as "technical bricoleurs"—all have contributed to a new mood in pre-service literature. They direct initial teacher education research away from simple one-factor frames of reference that are highly deterministic in character, and toward research that situates the future teacher as an active rather than a passive agent, making meaning out of the cultural forms that impinge on professional preparation. This means continually negotiating subject positions out of a particular set of enabling/constraining conditions.

The term *critical pedagogy* was increasingly used as a means of identifying commonalities in the educational stories generated out of radical/avant-garde critiques. The *critical* element was indeed perceived to be critical in countering the possibility that pre-service teachers might be socialized into accepting the social and economic inequalities in a class-based society (Zeichner & Teitelbaum, 1982, p. 100). Such writing drew on a range of literature generated in the 1970s by curriculum theorists (e.g., Apple, 1979), educational sociologists (e.g., Jencks, 1979), and political economists (e.g., Bowles & Gintis, 1976). This literature focused on the extent to which schools function to perpetuate existing inequalities in society and to legitimate current sets of institutional arrangements.

The term "pedagogy" was revitalized in the 1980s so as to be conceptually quite distinct from teaching as a set of behavioral techniques. Pedagogy sought to address the process of production and exchange that takes place in the interaction of teacher, learner, and the knowledge jointly produced (Lusted, 1986, p. 3). Critical writers insisted that such a concept refused the instrumentalization of these relations, highlighting instead "exchange between and over categories . . . recogniz [-ing] the productivity of the relations and . . . render[ing] the parties within them as active, changing and changeable agencies" (p. 3). In focusing on knowledge production in this way, pedagogical concerns were to draw attention to the conditions necessary to maximize opportunities for effecting appropriate change. In particular, such conceptualization of the role of education called attention to the power relations within which knowledge is produced.

The call to critical pedagogy has continued to challenge positivistic, ahistorical, and depoliticized analyses by liberal and conservative educational critics for their failure to engage or transform teachers. Founded on the conviction that schooling for self and social empowerment is ethically prior to a mastery of technical skills, its social justice agenda challenged liberal democratic emphases on individualism and the autonomy of rational conscious selves whose actions and decisions originate with themselves. The task, according to its advocates, was the development of a language of critique that facilitates an understanding of the means by which capitalism sustains unequal social relations (Giroux, 1983; McLaren, 1988). Human autonomy and self-transformation were held to be possible only when this social order is transformed. At the same time, individuals could develop subject positions from which to recognize "their true selves" (McLaren, 1988, p. 5). The pursuit of this "one true position" has been the cornerstone and the Achilles heel of the critical project.

An important epistemological item on this reconceptualist agenda was the assertion that science as embodied in the positivist "quantitative/qualitative" paradigm has failed to serve the best interests of teachers and teacher educators in its representation of the nature of teaching itself. At the heart of this challenge was the desire to elevate notions of "relevant teacher preparation" that are wedded to hermeneutic and critical paradigms of inquiry at the expense of positivism (Barrow, 1984; Giroux, 1981; Gore, 1987; Liston & Zeichner, 1987; O'Loughlin & Campbell, 1988).

Such reconceptualizations of teacher education emerged out of a long-term reorientation of inquiry into many fields of study: social sciences and professional studies in general as well as education (Schubert, 1989, p. 27). Far from representing tinkering with the dominant paradigms of inquiry, these challenges struck at the very beliefs and assumptions about relevant knowledge that have become the taken-for-granted of traditional research, including the vast bulk of that research which has informed teacher educational theory and practice.

Traditional teacher education research has been under attack for marginalizing epistemology and misrepresenting or trivializing interpretive inquiry through its emphasis on testability of concepts as "what counts" as information about human behavior. Traditionally, claims to knowledge, as opposed to opinion, have been validated as certain or unchallengeable because "they could be shown to follow by some procedure of rational inference from . . . epistemic foundations or to be foundational items themselves" (Walker, 1985, p. 56). This hegemonic principle is now being undermined.

It has been argued (e.g., Eisner, 1988; Giddens & Turner, 1987; Johnson, 1980) that the dominance of positivist research models in educational inquiry has elevated the "knower" to a separate and, importantly, an alienated status in terms of the known. Eisner's critique is typical:

> We talk about our findings implying somehow that we discover the world rather than construe it. . . . The motive . . . is found in our search for objectivity, that God's eye view of the world that sees comprehensively and without the encumbrances of feeling, motives, interests or a personal biography. We distance ourselves from the phenomena we wish to understand so that we can see then from the knee of God—or at least somewhere close by. (1988, p. 18)

The central problem is that theoretical absolutism and conceptions of cultural products (e.g., pedagogic discourse) as "nicely lying there, merely waiting analysis or appreciation" (Johnson, 1980, p. 6) trivialize the important tasks. To proceed on this basis, according to Wexler (1987), is to "deny the symbolic labor of the process of knowing and the socially organized processes through which representations are produced" (p. 83).

Insights of this kind called for a reassessment of the many studies of teachers and their work that have been founded on a positivist epistemology. Teacher socialization research in particular, such as that of Leggatt (1970), Lieberman (1956), McPherson (1972), and Simpson and Simpson (1969) has already been challenged. Its behaviorist bias allowed a disconcertingly unproblematic view of becoming a teacher, geared as it is to the production of definitive lists of competencies or traits to be developed in the novice. Such work is also attacked as providing merely an uncritical reiteration of professionals' pious hopes and self-interests (Roth, 1974). Further, it has been argued that such studies marginalize the "knowledgeability" of the social actors under scrutiny (Giddens & Turner, 1987, p. 226).

The tendency to work against teachers rather than with them, it has been argued, has produced a split between research and practice, because the production of "knowledge-as-standards" appears to pit the academic sector of the profession against the teaching sector (Sockett, 1987; Tripp, 1990). Further, such findings have appeared to serve the interests of those governing bodies that would seek to constrain teachers in terms of status and practice rather than to enable them.

Of critical importance, according to Wexler (1987, p. 31), is the extent to which such work is perceived as substituting correlations of abstracted variables for analyses of the socialization processes in teaching institutions and the role of broader contextual factors in shaping the cultural definitions of those outcomes. While appropriate for certain kinds of tasks, in particular the description and comparison of certain structural givens over time and place, it is regarded as inadequate in dealing with the medium of education itself. Basil Bernstein (1986, p. 205) explained this not as an oversight but as the inevitable result of research whose analyses assume or take for granted the very discourse that is subject to their analysis.

Bernstein was not alone in bemoaning the methodologically and theoretically restricted state of teacher education research and its failure to revitalize and invigorate teacher education in the 1980s (Bannister, 1981; Battersby & Ramsay, 1983; Bertaux & Kohli, 1984; Everton, Hawley, & Zlotnik, 1984; Lawn & Barton, 1985; Sprinthall & Theis-Sprinthall, 1983; Walker, 1985; Wexler, 1987). Accusations mounted about the perceived failure of teacher educators/researchers to address the process by which people may develop a capacity to think with or through their own theoretical perspectives. The dominance of positivist research was blamed for the extent to which teaching has remained imitative of tradition rather than transformative (O'Loughlin & Campbell, 1988, p. 55), and this phenomenon in turn was blamed by neoconservative writers for perceived crises in terms of a pervasive lack of higher-order thinking skills in schools (Cheney, 1987; Hirsch, 1987).

Now the entire terrain of debate is shifting. Lather (1991a, p. 8) cites Caputo (1987, p. 262) in making use of the term *postparadigmatic diaspora* to describe the extent to which epistemological certainties have been wrenched away from their moorings by postmodernist challenges to modernist narratives. Poststructuralist penetration of old binary formulations (e.g., science versus false consciousness, subject versus object, inside versus outside) has diffused research theory, disallowing much without indicating clear paths forward. Hebdidge elaborates on the challenge to the old order of critique:

> If the "depth model" disappears so, too, does the intellectual as seer, the intellectual as informed and dispassionate observer/custodian of a field of inquiry . . . there can be no more rectification of popular errors, no more trawling for hidden truths, no more going behind appearances or "against the grain" of the visible and the obvious. (1988, p. 192)

Teacher education has not yet been informed in any significant way by this epistemological shift. The binary structure through which positivism/antipositivism is understood as *the* logic of research rationality still holds a monopoly on the thinking that informs social research. Educational scholarship was for many years accused of being "idolatrously fixed on the measurable" (McLaren, 1986, p. 20). Much has changed. "Progressive" projects have become increasingly antistructuralist but this is not to be equated with antifoundational work. The radical feminist call to transcend "methodolatry" (Daly, 1973, cited in Lather, 1991a, p. 6) is a call not to do more qualitative studies but to disrupt the positivist/antipositivist binary formulation altogether.

This call to unsettle the antipositivist project does not represent a rejection of what critical pedagogical writing did in informing teacher education in the 1980s. It must be acknowledged that critical writing contributed important notions to the relevance debate, including the following:

- In general, the culture of teacher education has shown itself to be highly resistant to new ways of conceiving knowledge.
- Epistemological issues are fundamental to the relevance debate, and in particular, claims to value-free knowledge or neutral methodology must be addressed.
- Understandings that do not seek to bifurcate thinking and doing are most appropriate in reworking the knowledge base toward more powerful means of explaining teacher work.
- Issues of race, class, culture, gender, and ecology will continue to be marginalized while the teacher education curriculum is located in Eurocentric and androcentric knowledges and practices.
- With instrumentalist versions of a relevant knowledge base currently triumphant in teacher education policy, critical thought is most likely to be a casualty of change in moves toward a reformed curriculum, despite its "empowering" agenda.
- Since the social, political, and economic context in which educational work is being done is increasingly applying pressure to define teaching in technocratic ways, the task of redefining relevance in terms of social justice is an urgent one.
- Phenomenological and ethnographic work can focus on the language through which pre-service teachers give meaning to their experiences, on the linguistic context in which this occurs, and on the social relations of the research act itself. This assists in addressing the genuine problem of impoverished theory and method that has directly and indirectly contributed to the disempowerment of teachers.

The radical formulations of the nature of teacher work that critical pedagogues produced were meant to replace dull instrumentalism with a language of hope and transformation. Yet in damning teacher education culture as "ideological," the clear tales we told as critical pedagogues set in place in the literature a number of repressive myths. I was forced to acknowledge that pre-service teachers did not differentiate a critical agenda from other "academic" tales, except perhaps to discern that its vocabularies were often more difficult to access and its evangelism was at times more strident. In seeking to maintain a "pure" ideological position, critical teachers did not adequately explore the possibility that critical practices might operate repressively under certain local conditions. As a result, the "oppositional" work of social reconstructionists has not countered the lack of reflexivity in teacher education research overall. Indeed, it has abetted it. In particular, critical teacher educators failed to perceive the importance of specific contexts and local manifestations within which teacher education comes to be known (Gore, 1991, p. 49). The tendency was still to present "a moving and flowing network of practices and assumptions" (Terdiman, 1985, p. 57) as though they are constituted as a fixed and global "given."

DOING "CORRECTIVE" RESEARCH: A CASE STUDY IN DECONSTRUCTION

As a corrective to this, feminist poststructuralists draw on Foucault's understanding of power as "co-extensive with the social body" (1980, p. 142), circulating everywhere through changing rather than fixed points and axes. Foucault challenges socially critical discourse by noting both the potential of power to be other than repressive, and the potential of any discourse, emancipatory in intent or not, to become part of a technology of surveillance.

Drawing on poststructuralist theory, Lather (1989) describes a method of deconstructive inquiry that is helpful in providing reflexivity for critical teacher education texts. Deconstruction allows examination of the complicity of critical writing in the folkloric traditions of "speaking" students because it does not seek to weigh the "truth" of these texts. Instead, it reveals the logic of the particular practices of articulation out of which these versions of the truth have been legitimated, over other possible truths in the taken-for-granted world of teacher education. Lather's version of the deconstructive process allows inquiry into the role played by socially critical discourse itself in perpetuating this folklore. At the same time, it has purported to stand in opposition to the dominant technocratic tradition of teacher education.

For Lather (1989), deconstruction is "the postmodern equivalent of the dialectic" in that it allows examination of the constitutive effects of our uses of language through "permanent critique of our own texts as well as others" (p. 10). Textual deconstruction of the type that Lather elaborates aims at "a more generous critical cultural politics" emerging out of "the recognition of our own inevitable collusion with what we contest" (p. 7). This type of deconstructive work is therefore more self-consciously political in its aims than the work of French poststructuralists from which it draws, and in this sense it is typical of contemporary feminisms of difference (Grosz, 1990, p. 101).

Lather's (1989) account of deconstructive procedure involves three steps or stages in the reading of text. The initial task is the identification of the binary oppositions on which the argument within a text is structured. Then, by proceeding to displace the logic of the text by relocating the negative as the very condition of the positive, the way is opened for understanding the symbiotic nature of the relationship that exists between the oppositions of the text itself. The final stage of deconstruction is the creation of a new conceptual organization out of the binary logic of the transcended text, one that is "both and neither of the binary terms" (p. 9).

Critical pedagogy as a grand narrative has tended to conflate what it seeks to be distanced from, i.e., the apparently uncritical, the undertheorized, or the apolitical, into the Other of teacher education. This is achieved by writing from the margins of a "monolithic" instrumentalist orientation, one that ignores significant developments in current social theorizing, particularly in relation to matters of social justice.

The work of Smith and Zantiotis (1988a, 1988b) is a suitable case for deconstructive treatment as an exemplar of the "clear images" that avant-garde texts generate about who "we" are as critical pedagogues, and who "they" are as an opposing tradition of "others." Three qualities recommend their work to me for deconstruction. First, it is representative of a critique of teacher education that acknowledges the effects of discourse as embodied in the actual practices in the institutions, patterns of behavior, and forms of pedagogy within teacher education (Smith & Zantiotis, 1988b, p. 100). It is itself informed from a Foucauldian perspective while retaining, as is true of most avant-garde educational discourse, elements of "modernism." Second, and importantly, it exemplifies a view of teacher education with which I have much empathy: the urgent need for the development of "progressive pedagogies" that recontextualize the reality of schooling and realize counterdominant practices (p. 25). Third, the text's writing highlights the binary oppositions understood to exist in teacher education and so, to some extent, the deconstructive process is already under way in the text, albeit in reverse.

Smith and Zantiotis (1988a) speak of two discursive traditions within teacher education—the *dominant* and the *avant-garde*. The *dominant* they describe as "narrowly focussing on a specific kind of individualisation, technocratic effectiveness and co-ordination of schooling to fit the requirements of an emerging economic order" (p. 77). This discursive tradition, they argue, has the effect of making teaching "an instrumental activity" in which programs of teacher education lose sight of the "nexus of value, purpose and procedure" that makes up education and the social conditions in which it occurs (p. 77). The trend is being furthered by "the logic of the new market place" such that education itself is now "constituted as a commodity" (p. 79). For Smith and Zantiotis, the effects of the dominance of this tradition are that teacher education "subjects" are cued by means of a "discourse of practicality" that locates the "source of knowledge, skills, and attitudes for the production of knowledge about teaching" in "the objective relations of teaching in schools" (p. 85). While this discourse of practicality is neither internally coherent nor uncontested, it nevertheless frames judgments about teacher practice as "internal to the practicality of doing classroom work," thus having the effect of disallowing the contesting political nature of educational work (p. 85).

The *avant-garde*, on the other hand, is identified as:

> a "visionary" tradition, anchored in a genre of discourse that privileges the concepts of emancipation, liberation and democracy . . . intend[ing] to neutralise and exclude dominant teacher education discourse and to replace it with a language of possibility and hope. (p. 77)

The avant-garde attempts to problematize the "realist genre" of teacher education that arises out of the discourse of practicality, wherein teacher educators "are left with reinventing a sense of the past, with plagiarizing older plots and narratives to tell stories about teaching" (p. 87). The avant-garde tradition critiques both the dominance of positivistic psychological models of teaching and learning and the de-emphasis of pedagogical work (pp. 87–88) in teaching that is "instrumental and technique-centred" (p. 89). While Smith and Zantiotis note that criticisms of the avant-garde have and can be made (p. 93), they assert that it is the avant-garde that has the capacity to shape and critically inform knowledge positions in critical pedagogy and to "enable student teachers to engage with their own and their students' subject positions and schooling" (p. 96).

Smith and Zantiotis go on to argue that a symbiotic relationship exists between avant-garde and dominant discursive practices of teacher education. The avant-garde "takes on alien elements of the dominant in its attempts to overcome them" just as the dominant must look to absorbing and thereby extinguishing the avant-garde by recuperating its attempts at subversion and striving for coherence in order to maintain the "normal" or "established order" in teacher education (p. 82). What they and other critical pedagogues fail to do is to make a problem out of the clarity of their own binary formulation to allow a more reflexive moment in their critique. This means recognizing "the necessity with which what a text says is bound up with what it cannot say" (Grosz, 1990, p. 97).

Despite subversive intent, the complicity of the pedagogical practices of avant-garde educators in ensuring that the dominant remains so must now be acknowledged as a real possibility, once avant-garde textual logic is decentered. Indeed, for tertiary students it is more likely that this binary system is actually experienced as a discordant cacophony of "expert" voices rather than as contesting educational ideologies.

These contestations and accommodations are played out in an ongoing way within the texts that pre-service teachers generate about their own needs. The discursive traditions constitute the context that shapes what can be meaningfully articulated in the relevance debate, not only by pre-service teachers but also by teacher educators. Furthermore, all of this struggle is also shaped by, and continuously responsive to, the rationalizing discursive framework of postwelfare capitalism.

Smith and Zantiotis's (1988a) analysis sets up a binary opposition in which the avant-garde, though acknowledged as existing in a symbiotic relationship with the dominant discursive tradition, is understood as the positive term. In order to deconstruct this binary opposition, we need to generate new terminology that functions in such a way as to move the negative term, in this case the dominant discursive tradition, from its oppositional role into the very heart of the positive term, the avant-garde tradition. It is this process that reveals "the necessity with which what a text says is bound up with what it cannot say" (Grosz, 1990, p. 97).

The terminology generated by Fraser's work (1989) is again of assistance here because Fraser's analytical framework provides new vocabularies that allow us to transcend the binary categorizations "avant-garde" and "dominant" without denying the fundamentally political nature of the contestation over needs. In the process of generating more fluid categorizations after decentering the logic of the text in order to displace the primacy of avant-garde over dominant, we can make use of Fraser's *needs talk* categorizations, in particular her use of the term *expert needs talk*. The term "expert" is an appropriate hinge word, one that is simultaneously both and neither of these categorizations, but well suited in terms of the perspectives of pre-service teachers. From their "bottom-up" point of view, both dominant and avant-garde discourse may be undifferentiated as teacher educator "expertise" that ought to be critiqued when failing to produce expert practices. The extent to which their courses are terrains of ideological struggle may simply be experienced as lecturers who "can't get their [collective] act together," or who are "so heavenly minded that they're no earthly good." This is especially so if the pedagogy through which "teacher knowledge" is disseminated appears hierarchical, monologic, sterile, or laissez-faire.

In that socially critical discourse is self-consciously "oppositional," avant-garde writers may well hold that Fraser's categorization *oppositional needs talk* best describes Smith and Zantiotis's avant-garde teacher education discourse, in that it has "a relativising and estranging effect . . . (which is) . . . subversive of normality and . . . heterodox" (Smith & Zantiotis, 1988b, p. 82). However, for pre-service teachers struggling to make sense of a program in which so many struggles for legitimacy are being conducted between departments and institutions, it is more likely to remain undifferentiated as another potentially disempowering expert voice. This is particularly so if the language of critical pedagogy remains inaccessible and the agenda is construed by them as negative.

While pre-service programs continue to service and be serviced by departments of psychology, sociology, philosophy, and curriculum, and while ideological debates that pre-service teachers remain unaware of or are catapulted into rage within and across these, it is hard to imagine any clarity emerging out of the chatter of "expert" voices talking at students. The advice of the supervising teacher at the school where the practicum is conducted may be a welcome escape from this chatter.

If pre-service teachers are understood as generating their own resistance (*oppositional needs talk*) rather than merely being overpowered by the dominant discursive tradition, then it might also be possible to understand the part played by critical discourse differently. The critical role is now open to be critiqued as one among many forms of *expert talk,* in Fraser's (1989) terms, rather than as the true politicizing voice. In applying Fraser's framework, I have made problematic the notion of resistance in teacher education discourse. It can now be understood as students' "talking back," as "defiant speech" reminiscent of that constructed within minority communities as a condition of survival (Ellsworth, 1989, p. 310).

NEW ACCOUNTS OF DIFFERENCE IN PRE-SERVICE TEACHERS

In drawing on Fraser's (1989) terminology, then, it is possible to interrupt and displace the binary strategies of avant-garde text. This allows analysis of student talk about their own professional needs as something new and potentially powerful, not just an echo of dominant discourse. In the case of my own work, it allowed me to proceed with the sort of analyses that appear in the following chapters of this book.

In intervening in this deconstructionist way in our own categorizations, we can generate new and more powerful understandings of pre-service teacher texts as discourse created out of the politics of needs interpretation. These texts become an appropriately "defiant speech" on the discursive terrain of pre-service teacher education, oppositional to the way their subjectivities are shaped by both the collusion and contestation of avant-garde and dominant discourses. Pre-service texts can now be read as real critiques of teacher education needs talk, not the products of false consciousness. Such insights into our own understanding may challenge perceptions of pre-service teachers as "unfortunately" clinging to the technical at the expense of more perceptive political critiques and force teacher educators to address more honestly the issue of the fallibility of our own pedagogy in action.

Curthoys (1988, p. 83) draws attention to this problem in her critique of the disorganization and defensiveness of contemporary radical politics and the extent to which its discourse has disallowed questioning the unquestionable. As examples of these repressive myths in avant-garde teacher education I would cite the way issues of technique have been reconstructed in much of the literature of critical pedagogy. Calls for better technique have been viewed as synonymous with demands to provide a list or recipe of "do's and don'ts," which is managerial and narrowly prescriptive. The very word "technique" has become anathema in the literature, and this has contributed in no small way to the bifurcation of theory and practice on the teacher education site. Yet pre-service teachers' negating responses to socially critical discourse and its silences about the "how to" is not necessarily the hallmark of a narrow technocratic rationality (McWilliam, 1992). It is understandable that pre-service teachers need technique to be able to "play out critique in the real" in their own teaching (Foucault, 1981, p. 13). In conflating technique with technicism, critical pedagogues concede "doing" to behaviorists, managerialists, or curriculum specialists.

A further problem for avant-garde teacher educators continues to be the unrelieved pessimism of critical pedagogy. In attempting to counter the naive and seductive simplicity of behaviorist propositions in teacher education, socially critical teachers have become captives of their own determination to initiate student teachers into a world of

educational injustice. Despite the rhetoric of "hope" and "transformation," the anxious messages of critical pedagogy are more likely to be
received in "councils of despair" (Simon, 1988, p. 4) during classes
of sociology or philosophy. Critical teacher educators are increasingly
perceived as conveying little more than a litany of complaints about
the very sort of contemporary practice student teachers have to imitate,
at least to some extent, in the field component of their preparation.
Talk often oscillates between advocacy of student autonomy-as-
democracy in learning and a sort of evangelistic demand that students
acknowledge and repent any lack of identification with critical
agendas. The call to social justice can so easily be construed as lefter-
than-thou superiority or dubious moral heroics in these circumstances.

Ellsworth's (1989) concerns about this phenomenon in the practices of antiracist pedagogy are well known. From the luxury of my
vantage point in a school whose credentials in critical pedagogy were
well established, I have also been moved to reflect on the number of
apparently empathic young women in my own and other classes who
claim to have been bullied for their lack of devotion to the cause of
feminist studies. I have felt decidedly uneasy about the very ease with
which this was dismissed by my colleagues as backlash politics. Real
feminist teachers could not be putting them off, it was argued. Real
feminist pedagogy doesn't go off the rails in this way, they said. This
was a misreading or another small l liberal agenda trying to reassert
itself.

I know that women, including academics, are pilloried for behavior that is deemed justified or natural in men as white middle-class
reformers, including top-down pedagogy. But I remained uneasy
about the fact that as feminists we submitted other teachers to more
rigorous critiques than we were prepared to make of ourselves.

By means of this logic, avant-garde educators remain complicit in
the very discursive order that they oppose, despite binary formulations
of socially critical work as separate from, and antithetical to, "dominant" traditions. Students were to blame for their failure to accept liberating versions of the truth about relevant professional preparation.
The effect of these discursive practices would be that critical teacher
educators "misrecognized" themselves as empowering agents. In constructing an adversary that was always external to critical discourse—
a dominant/technocratic tradition of teacher education—critical pedagogy failed to allow space for within/against critique (Lather, 1991a).

Poststructuralists' refusal to settle on a new regime requires a new
respect for the notion of disruptive experiment, of playful research. We
need to get serious about play. This reforming tale is a part of such a

project. It does not argue that teacher educators (including academics involved in the project who eschew the title) ought to be reinstated in their rightful place in the scheme of things. Nor is it simply a defense of revamped critical pedagogy as the legitimate heir to the teacher education project. The point is that whoever become heirs to the project need more power than is generated by the folkloric discursive traditions of this present generation of teacher educators, and that includes the avant-garde scholarship of social reconstructionists.

CHAPTER 4

Slow and Sharp
Reconstructing Pre-service Teacher Socialization

WRITING PRE-SERVICE TEACHERS: BEYOND THE BINARIES

The following tale continues the theme that different methodological frameworks can make different sense of teacher education research data. It is my reworking of the simplistic proposition that pre-service teacher socialization can broadly be understood as a progression from *idealism to realism* or *humanism to custodialism*. I wanted to respond to Zeichner's call for greater understanding of "the interactions between individual intent and institutional constraint" in educational research (1986, p. 32). Given that these interactions are played out in the languages institutions make available to individuals (as well as the language personal biography has already provided), the focus of the study is the changing patterns of language use in the pre-service teachers who were my research subjects. My story is not dependent on attitudinal surveys, one-shot interviews, or pre or post questionnaires. It is generated out of a longitudinal study of the ways that pre-service teachers tell about their own needs and reflect on these scripts over the duration of their pre-service course.

This tale differs from many other models of narrative research in that, while it is focused on identity formation, the data are not in the form of life histories, nor is the analysis informed by linguistic or literary theory to any significant extent. Instead, it focuses on the contradictions and changes that are apparent in brief and extended texts, written and oral, generated by 14 pre-service teachers over three years. These texts are understood, within a socio-political framework, as particular forms of "defiant speech" (Ellsworth, 1989). My role as a researcher is to press the metaphors that appear in the student texts to construct my own more complex story of teacher socialization. Again, the point of constructing such a story is not to "disprove" findings about anticipatory or other forms of teacher socialization, but to contribute to and revitalize impoverished debate about the nature of teacher socialization. The purpose of the narrative is to display the unity and coherence, as well as the fragmentation and contradictions, of pre-service teacher texts as discursive events.

The tale proceeds from the assumption that pre-service teachers may be examined, in certain respects, as an oppressed community, at least in terms of their experience of professional knowledge on university campuses and during field experience. The extent to which pre-service teachers are silenced by the voices of the pedagogue and the supervisor and the "domesticating" effects of this "culture of silence" are reminiscent of the marginalization of voices in oppressed cultures that Freire (1973, 1985) has described and worked against. Beauchamp and Parsons' depiction of pre-service teachers certainly appears to support the appropriateness of this analogy:

> The student teacher is operating in a situation which almost demands him or her to hide, rather than reveal, his or her true feelings, beliefs and personality. (1989, p. 168)

What is important here is that the pre-service teacher is silent not in the sense of "having no voice," but rather in the sense of having no context in which the dissenting voice is legitimated. Feminists in particular have taken up the issue of "the fiction of the silence of subordinated groups" (Ellsworth, 1989, p. 313) in their own examinations of the power of patriarchy. The struggle of women of color, for example, has been not from silence to speech, but changing the nature and direction of that speech to more enabling political ends (hooks, 1989, p. 124).

As a teacher educator wishing to challenge my students to resist oppression in all its forms, I had a number of urgent questions about pre-service teacher socialization that I sought to probe through an examination of the way pre-service teachers talked about their professional educational needs. What language did students use to talk about their needs on entry to pre-service courses? In what ways did needs vocabularies change over the period of pre-service preparation? What similarities and differences were evident among individuals? Do pre-service teacher texts provide evidence of a hegemonic struggle over "legitimate" needs and, if so, how is this manifest?

BEYOND "ATTITUDE": THEORIZING PRE-SERVICE TEACHER TALK

Rather than attempt to engage with the voices of pre-service teachers through the language they themselves might choose, teacher education researchers have tended to rely on pre-service teacher reactions to the language of the researcher, for reasons of efficiency or perceived scientific rigor. The allocation of the student voice to "further comments" is the usual "post hoc" indication of the status such remarks are likely to have in the study—embellishment, not substance. Not only has teacher education research been unsystematic in the broad sense (Price, 1989, p. 22), but its very systems have denied the complexity, contradiction, and richness of student language.

For Ellsworth (1989), educational researchers must focus on attempting to construct meaningful discourses about the politics of educational practices "by theorizing the ways in which knowledge, power and desire are mutually implicated" (p. 316) in the formulations and deployments of those involved. She speaks of the need for pedagogues who, "as the privileged speaking/making subject," work "to unlearn that privilege" by responding to subjugated knowledges among their own groups of students (p. 323), and helping them to name, fight, and survive forms of pedagogical oppression (p. 318). Part of this agenda is the recovery of student language as a defiant speech, while at the same time understanding it as a partial narrative in keeping with our own.

While Ellsworth's theorizing of student voices as defiant speech draws attention to the micro-politics of the classroom and is also directly applicable to the practicum experience, Fraser's conceptualizing of "the politics of need interpretation" (1989, p. 163) theorizes the struggle over welfare needs in a way that is useful in constructing a new socialization tale. Given that the focus is on analyzing how pre-service teachers perceive their own needs, and how this changes over time, Fraser's understanding of "needs talk" as both political and politicizing allows the complexity of pre-service needs to be more fully explored (p. 169). As I have already indicated, her analysis of the "struggle for hegemonic needs interpretations" in late capitalist society (p. 173) can be meaningfully applied to struggles over educational needs, and in particular, as they are played out in microcosm in local teacher education settings.

Fraser's (1989) conceptualization of *oppositional needs talk*—with its potential for the creation of new and resistant social identities and its vulnerability, in embryonic form, to culturally dominant interpretations—may now prove a more fruitful framework for analysis of pre-service needs talk than positivistic analyses of "attitudinal" checklists. Fraser understands the power of dominant discourses to depoliticize fragmented, subcultural defiant speech, by means of the construction of "discursive enclaves" that legitimate certain official vocabularies and deny the legitimacy of others (p. 169). Yet she also speaks of "leaky" or "runaway" needs that have the potential to generate alternative vocabularies and to challenge dominant discourses (p. 169).

In order to apply Fraser's theorizing of the struggle over needs more fully to teacher education, we must identify the discursive enclaves that both generate and reflect the dominant discursive traditions of teacher education. As elaborated in Chapter 3, Smith and Zantiotis (1988a, 1988b) speak of a "discourse of practicality" as the dominant tradition, that is, the taken-for-granted or normal. This discourse privileges the immediate, the particular, and the concrete conditions and events in classrooms. Its metaphors construct teaching as constrained by organizational structures, including the need for control. Smith and Zantiotis argue that it is through such discourse that teacher work is framed in ways that ensure education functions as an ideological state apparatus (1988b, p. 84).

While Smith and Zantiotis's argument takes account of the dominance of instrumentalist/behaviorist models of teaching and learning in teacher education programs, it does not acknowledge the importance of another discursive tradition from which the "practicality" ethic in teacher text derives its power. As a teacher educator, I began to perceive an apparent pre-service teacher preference for romantic humanistic vocabularies in talking about educational work. "Raising self-esteem" seemed to be a central tenet of this "discourse of therapy," which had the effect of constructing student/clients as "ailing" or educationally fragile individuals who need the maternal care of teachers. Its driving logic seemed to be a social pathology model of both educational and interpersonal ill health, a model that, it has been argued, privileges the language of "legitimate labelers" such as doctors, psychiatrists, psychologists, and educators. Meighan elaborates on this:

> Such a model [of social pathology] employs quasi-medical terms like examination, diagnosis, treatment and testing, and proves to be convenient for . . . those teachers who think in medically derived terms. Excluded by such an approach are the possibilities that causes outside the biographies of the individual, such as the regime of the school, the expectations of the teachers, or the ideology of the education in use, may be crucial factors. (1981, p. 323)

While those entering pre-service may not have access to the expert needs talk (Fraser, 1989) of professional health workers, they certainly appeared to have ready access to "therapy talk" through popularized versions that abound in late capitalist culture. A whole discursive tradition that has pervaded seminars training "one-minute-managers" in "good interpersonal and communication skills" has incorporated a therapeutic or "counseling" vocabulary as a legitimate part of its language. This "language of therapy," linked discursively to a narcissistic "cult of self," is also evident in popular forms of entertainment, from magazines to soap operas. Like its parent language of social pathology, it constructs individuals as free and responsible for their own destiny, yet "lacking" and therefore "in need of" vital skills that, if mastered, will mean social success. The problem with the rationale of this language is that, in broad terms, individual biography is the sole cause of social "illness," and the sole source of future social transformation.

In seminar discussions, I noted that pre-service teachers absolved themselves from any complicity in oppressive classroom practices through reiterating their commitment to "cater to individual differences," to "raise self-esteem," or "to help students reach their full potential." They saw themselves as actively working for social justice and against authoritarianism in their commitment to these goals. It seemed to me, then, that the construction and regulation of the relationship between managerial discourses and discourses of therapy demanded much more attention from teacher educators/researchers. The metaphor of "parent discourses" seemed apposite, in that these discourses appeared to exist as "father/mother" to "embryonic" or "infant" discourses brought by pre-service teachers to teacher education sites, in terms of their effects as a discursive regime.

My own analysis (which is elaborated below) strongly suggests that a paternal "discourse of managerial efficiency" works in tandem with the kinder maternal face of the "discourse of therapy" to recuperate potentially "runaway" educational needs discourse (Fraser, 1989). The power of these dominant discourses, I would argue, is that, in symbiosis, they have a capacity to rework a potentially political language of resistance into a romantic discourse about the self. This is achieved by means of vocabularies that rework educational injustice as a problem of "disruption" to be responded to with more "control," a problem of "individual emotional need" to be responded to with therapy and psychology, or a combination of both. In contemporary schools, "disruptive" students can be found oscillating between the offices of the principal and the school psychologist. Moreover, there are any number of labels that may now be applied to their "condition" that may explain why they are unteachable.

The construction of "teacher-as-technicist," accommodating while contesting "teacher-as-therapist," militates against pre-service teachers' exploring the complicity of both in shaping pedagogical work. Each parent discourse contributes to this process by generating and sustaining highly individualizing vocabularies for the articulation of "legitimate talk" about professional needs. "Equity" demands are most successfully recuperated when paternal concerns with "standards," "merit," and "excellence" are mediated by maternal concerns for "raising individual self-esteem." What emerges is a depoliticization of "equity," which is now couched as an "individual performance/ remediation" issue. In this view, any broader contextual conceptualization must lead to forms of social engineering antithetical to individual excellence. Alternative educational understandings could not allow for the proper differentiation of merit.

The dominance of these discursive forms in pre-service teacher education does not, of course, preclude other discursive elements from informing and regulating the languages used by those who participate in it. The role of critical pedagogy, for example, has been to deny forms of personal power that derive from the individual psychology and circumstances of human agents (Miller, 1990, p. 123). Other discursive systems, such as those that pertain to particular subject disciplines, also have a regulative effect. Vocabularies that construct the teaching of business studies, for example, are in many ways very different from those constructing the teaching of drama. "Knowledge-as-content" is articulated in ways that are not necessarily regulated by the same language "rules" as "knowledge-as-process." The ongoing impact of popular discourse about teaching and teachers is also implicated in the construction of needs discourse. "Commonsense" articulations of teacher work have the potential to *re*form teaching practices by marginalizing pedagogical matters in favor of minimalist notions of competence, narrowly defined.

Apart from the above-mentioned, an unlimited array of discourses can shape the language any individual may use to articulate professional and personal needs. Biography is in itself so complex that a researcher could not hope to identify all the possible languages available to subjects. Yet the task ought not to be understood as a "teasing out" of vocabularies into distinct linguistic "pieces" of a discursive jigsaw puzzle. Lather's (1993, p. 16) image of a rhizomatic "journey among intersections" seems a more appropriate analogy.

THE METAPHOR AS THE MESSAGE:
RECONSTRUCTING STUDENT TALES

My tale is constructed out of texts provided by 14 undergraduates over the three-year period of their initial teacher education course. Out of an original group of 20, 6 were lost through attrition over the three years. The original 20 were chosen at random from a possible 72 on the basis of representative characteristics. The group not only spanned a range of subject disciplines, but also represented both females and males, mature age and school leavers, and rural and urban dwellers.

Each participant provided five pieces of extended writing (including three statements about their professional needs), one at the beginning of each year of pre-service (literally written on the first day of the undergraduate course), and two at the beginning of the action phase of the research (i.e., the start of their final semester). Each participant was also interviewed about perceived differences and similarities in the first two written texts in the middle of second year. In this way, the "thick" data generated in written texts well before and after the first field experience could be analyzed and explained by the participants themselves. In this interactive interview, participants analyzed the continuities and discontinuities they noted between their first and second "needs talk" texts. A very important issue for the researcher here was the extent to which any potentially "oppositional needs talk" evident in the texts generated on entry had already been recuperated by the dominant discourses of teacher education described above.

The written texts done at the beginning of each year responded to the same discursive tasks every year. At the start of each of their pre-service years the research participants were required to complete three statements that began in the following ways:

- Secondary teachers need to know . . .
- Secondary teacher education should therefore involve . . .
- I expect what I will be learning here will be . . .

These statements were designed to gather information not only about the construction of pre-service discourse about "legitimate" teacher work, but also the matter of the "fit" between the pre-service course design and versions of "relevant teacher knowledge" generated by the participants themselves. What I hoped to explore through these extended statements was the relationship between the discursive construction of teaching and the versions of curriculum relevance that are shaped by competing versions of "teacher needs" struggling for hegemonic articulation in the text.

The participants wrote their responses each time without viewing the responses they made the previous year. However, they perused their first two responses at length in order to provide the oral text generated in the second-year interview. Further, the participants were provided with the three written texts and the one oral text they had generated when completing the fourth and fifth pieces of extended writing, which led into the "reflection-in-action" research phase. These consisted of responses to the following two topics:

- How my understanding of my needs as a teacher has changed over three years.
- What I now believe I need.

These two parts of the final phase of data gathering for discourse analysis allowed me as researcher to "check" my own understandings of patterns that appeared to emerge against those provided by the individuals in the group about themselves. It also allowed group participants to reflect on their entire course in order to provide both researcher and researched with an appropriate knowledge base to negotiate a "relevant-needs" curriculum in the last semester.

The analysis of the "interpretive discourse" provided by the 14 participants proceeds along the lines suggested by Mishler (1990), in that the texts written and spoken by particular individuals over time are reconceptualized as instances of more abstract and general types of texts, that is, how this type of student needs talk constructs through metaphor a particular version of the nature of teaching as work. What characterizes these texts and allows them to be differentiated is elaborated, and the "structure" of relationships among texts is explored. Finally, the "meaning" of this structure in terms of what it provides to challenge more orthodox research on pre-service contributions to the socialization process will be addressed.

In applying Fraser's (1989) notion of oppositional needs talk to student texts, I wanted initially to examine the language students used on entry into the course as a basis for a progressive political project. To what extent did the needs interpretations of these university entrants "closely approximate ideals of democracy, equality and fairness" (p. 182)? Or had the students already rewritten themselves in an idiom that militated against a progressive educational politics by passively framing themselves, and thereby their own future students, as "candidates for state-organized provision" (p. 173)?

Because incoming undergraduates already have a long history of involvement in educational institutions and therefore with forms of institutional knowledge production and utilization, I felt it would be unlikely that their initial needs talk would be a "self-constituted" moment as is characteristic of oppositional discourses (Fraser, 1989, p. 171). Yet their very status as students had within it the potential to generate forms of defiant speech that might be much more geared to democratic educational ideals than teacher educator researchers have as yet acknowledged.

FIRST-YEAR STORIES

To pursue this further, I attempted to probe discursive elements that had the potential to either open up or shut down progressive possibilities in student needs talk. To do this, I attended to the metaphorical characteristics of the first texts written on entry to the teacher education course. This strategy was based on the assumption that all language is ineradicably metaphorical and that metaphor is essentially groundless, "merely substituting one set of signs for another" (Sarup, 1988, p. 51). I assumed that theories are inextricably linked to metaphor (Gottlieb, 1989, p. 136), which, in turn, are related to asymmetrical social relations and the organization of power. Thompson's understanding of the role of language, as elaborated below, was therefore central to this analysis:

> We are constantly involved in extending the meaning of words, in producing new meanings through metaphor, word-play and interpretation; and we are thereby also involved, knowingly or not, in altering, undermining or reinforcing our relations with others and with the world. (1984, p. 6)

Analyzing metaphorical language about the nature of teacher work would allow detection of the point at which pre-service teacher language, like any other, tends to betray its own fictional and arbitrary nature at the same time that it is at its most intensely persuasive.

Egalitarian, two-way metaphors for the teaching and learning process were dominant in the first-year texts. In these initial texts, the teaching/learning experience was depicted in spatial and relational metaphors that were, with some exceptions, close, supportive, and horizontal. "How to communicate" is clearly an important organizing signifier around which these metaphors are generated. What is identifiable is that "able to communicate" is articulated in early texts as a two-way process of horizontal exchange, not simply as a process of vertical "relay" or "transfer." Metaphors situate the teacher-as-communicator "beside" and "behind," not simply "in front of," students, while students are generally depicted as the focus of the teaching act. Examples include communicating "on an equal level basis"; "able to teach not dictate"; "students to be able to express themselves freely"; "how to think like each and every student they teach"; "being able to talk and communicate with students so that there becomes a mutual trust or friendship." Some writers provided extended egalitarian metaphors that stressed the democratic rights of students to question content and process:

> Because so many students (I did myself) ask "Why do we have to know this?" or "How can I use this in a job?" I also think teachers should remember that they themselves were students once and had similar crises and problems and feelings! (Andrea[1])

> Teachers need to know how to encourage learning, rather than how to teach "parrot fashion." Students need to know WHY they are learning a particular subject, and therefore teachers will need to know where a particular topic is likely to lead, and most important, what success is likely to mean to the student in the outside world. (Ken)

> If a teacher understands his/her students' hopes and aspirations, then he/she can help the student more than if they just walked in, read the class work content and left without getting any input from their students. (Trevor)

> Secondary teachers should also learn to encourage each student and not to practice favoritism [as this only demoralizes students]. (Mandy)

It would be hard to argue with the proposition that this "student-centered" orientation has a great deal to do with their own status, in that many of the writers are recent school leavers and all are first-year undergraduates. Nevertheless, the image of teacher as engaged in "friendly dialogue" with students has much to recommend it in terms of critical pedagogy. Working in close proximity in an egalitarian environment of sharing knowledge in the way that is suggested above is certainly akin to the pedagogical practices of Freirean models of teaching, for example.

In teacher socialization literature (e.g., Fuller, 1969; Gehrke & Yamamoto, 1978; Hoy, 1969; McArthur, 1981), this type of discourse has been understood as a manifestation of student "idealism" or "humanism," and has remained undifferentiated from other discursive elements such as forms of "therapy talk" that tend to construct teaching as a form of therapeutic service. What is important is the oppositional or avant-garde potential that exists in the egalitarian, dialogic elements of the needs talk cited above, as distinct from the heavily psychologized and depoliticizing therapy talk with which it has been conflated in the teacher education literature.

Elements of the latter are also present in the needs-talk data of this research. Student learners are also constructed at times as educationally ill and requiring remediation. In this sort of text, mutual images of working "with" are replaced by more distancing images of working "on." The notion of working for the good of the individual is nevertheless maintained, though many students are now differentiated as failures. Examples include "giving the students the knowledge they need with the personal touch"; "teach effectively for students of all academic ability (e.g., what to do when there are slower learners in a majority of quick learners or vice versa)"; "how to encourage slow learners, some special teaching skills as many [students are] disabled [physical and mental]"; "some Special Ed., perhaps aimed at deaf, etc."; "various teaching methods for the various types of students (smart, average, etc.)." Again, there were also some extended passages that exemplified the regulatory power of this discourse of therapy:

> I think also that there should be a course that will help new teachers understand each student especially those with some problem. Such as helping a child who may have domestic problems at home, find a place at school where they can enjoy themselves and be glad to be there. Hope you can understand what I mean! I also think learning about adolescene [sic] and adolescents; the way they in general function, think etc is a good idea. Also some study of psycology [sic] is a good idea also I think. (Marilyn)

> Teachers should also be very aware of the problems faced by their teenage students and how to deal with them. Teachers need to be sensitive to the situations many of their students find themselves in. . . . I don't believe that someone can to [sic]

taught how to be a teacher but the natural teaching skills within individuals should be encouraged to develop. (Melanie)

What is particularly noteworthy about the discursive fragments identified above as informed by a dominant discourse of therapy is the extent to which they are written in close proximity to managerial or "custodial" talk. The metaphor of teaching as a type of "balancing" between the requirements of these two apparently contradictory elements is significant in terms of earlier discussion of the power of the symbiotic relationship that exists between therapy talk and managerial discourse. This is not only apparent here, but is a theme of many texts over the entire time span of the research. Examples from pre-service first-year texts include "how to control and keep a class interested"; "giving the students the knowledge they need with the personal touch"; "being able to absorb and pass on information in an informative way"; "know what you really want them to know or think about and how to make it as simple and interesting as possible"; "some teachers . . . unable to find a happy medium between having the students' respect and having a comfortable relationship with them"; "learning how to take control of a classroom as well as making it a comfortable enviroment [sic]."

The extended passage below uses the metaphor of "line drawing" rather than "finding a happy medium" to indicate the importance of this need for balance or for "equal territory" between teacher-as-therapist and teacher-as-manager. Further, the metaphor "air of mystery" serves a spatial function in the text as distancing teacher from learner. Finally, the metaphor of "dealing with" learners and their problems is a one-way, top-down image of teachers' work. In this text, all the spatial metaphors through which the teacher/learner relationship is articulated have the effect of distancing teacher from learner, despite the superficially progressive rhetoric:

[Secondary teachers need to know] how to communicate with adolescents on a teacher/student level. I feel teachers can become too familiar with their students and a line must be drawn. The best teachers are those with some sort of "air of mystery" surrounding them. Students shouldn't need to know the ins and outs of their teachers' private lives. Teachers should be very aware of the problems faced by their teenage students and how to deal with them. Teachers need to be

sensitive to the situations many of their students find themselves in. (Melanie)

The above textual fragment provides an example of therapeutic and
managerial discourses as a mutually reinforcing or inhering discursive
couplet. Rather than describing pre-service teachers as moving from
humanistic/idealistic/"soft" attitudes to custodial/realistic/"hard"
ones, a more useful rearticulation becomes possible. If the written texts
of pre-service teachers on entry contain a host of discursive elements,
including oppositional, therapeutic, and managerial fragments, then
tracing the configurations and combinations of these vocabularies in
terms of their change over time and across individuals may yield a
more complex and revealing understanding of the role of pre-service
in teacher socialization than has been possible in previous studies.

The practice of conceptualizing pre-service teachers as simply
"changing their attitudes" over the duration of their course constrains
understanding of the complexity of teacher socialization. Not only
does it fail to differentiate potential discourses of resistance in initial
students' discursive practices, but it also fails to acknowledge that both
therapeutic discourse and managerial discourse are present to varying
degrees in first-year texts, serving the same hegemonic function within
the text through very different vocabularies. One could argue, then,
that it does not really matter whether student managerial or therapy
talk is labeled "realistic" or "idealistic," since both sets of discursive
practices, in various combinations, are serving the same ideological
ends. Rather, fragments of student discourse that can be co-opted for
the reconstruction of a politics of teaching and learning ought to be
actively differentiated from, not conflated with, a depoliticizing language of therapy. Noting the "play of surfaces" among these discursive
fragments might be a means by which my own critical pedagogy could
be informed and reconstructed at the pre-service level. I was also very
interested to examine differences and similarities that might emerge
in texts generated in the second year of training. How might these pre-
service teachers account for any differences and similarities?

SECOND-YEAR STORIES

The second-year texts provided a richer source of imagery and of
data, in that participants not only responded to the same written task
at the beginning of the tertiary year, but also engaged individually in
an oral interview to elaborate and discuss the differences and similarit-

ies between the two texts they had written. These interviews took place in late February and early March of 1990. By this time, the students had not only completed one full year of tertiary study toward their teaching qualification, but had engaged in a period of teaching practicum during the previous August. Rather than replicate the "pre- and postprac models" of the past, this research attempted to analyze more enduring discursive changes, many of which may have resulted from their experience of the practicum.

A noteworthy feature of the second-year texts was that, in many cases, the metaphors generated by the organizing signifier "how to communicate" had changed in terms of their spatial and interactional nature. The teacher/student relationship was now more noticeably hierarchical, with the teacher "standing in front of the class"; "maintaining professional distance"; "in charge in the classroom"; "giv[ing] a command knowing that the students will understand it and do it"; "up there teaching." Communication was now articulated through one-way metaphors that differentiated teachers and students horizontally and vertically. Two-way streets appeared to give way to one-way transmissions. The act of teaching was now "get[ting] the message across"; "get[ting] the point across"; "convey[ing] it to the students." Yet the notion of "balance" was maintained by elaborations such as the following:

> What I'm saying is if you can get your point across to the students by making it relevant for them and making it as interesting and as simple for them to understand as possible, then you've done your job as a teacher. (Andrea)

> You can still get your point across to adolescents but have them enjoy what you're saying. Like you're not speaking in a language that's over and above them. (Rita)

> And also to bring out a balance so you're not a total softie the way they can run over you, but you're not a tyrant where they won't listen to you 'cos you're an authoritative figure. More so like you're there to guide them but you're there to teach them as well. (Dee)

In some cases, the struggle for balance appeared already lost in favor of a more judgmental language of custodialism:

> Some people are bitchy toward other people but I like everyone and I feel that it is important that, as a teacher, you should

like everyone *even if they are the ratbag of the class or whatever.*
(emphasis added) (Trevor)

In other cases, the metaphor of balance was maintained through
an understanding of "presence," as a means to achieve simultaneous
"authority" over and "relationship" with students:

> You've got to make your presence felt in the classroom and
> start to feel everyone else out and know what they're on about
> so you can get that professional authority as a teacher over
> the students and them getting to know you and you getting
> to know them and getting a good working relationship going,
> good atmosphere in the classroom. And then, if you get that,
> you probably won't have even have to worry much about dis-
> cipline in general. (John)

An interesting metaphor that emerged in many second-year texts,
including the example above, is a metaphor of manual control or manipulation. Mention was made of "handling of certain situations"; the
need for "hands on experience"; "[knowing] how to handle students
in difficult situations"; "my ability to handle curriculum material";
"feel[ing] everyone else out"; or, alternatively, not being "prepared
enough to handle the situation or control it." "Lack of control" as understood and experienced in the prac situation is expressed through
this same metaphor, as a problem that "gets out of hand":

> I think if you've got a problem before it's too big, it's not a big
> problem. So you've got to be aware of what's going on all the
> time. You've sort of got to be watching everybody and it's
> easier to look at somebody and stop a problem than to let
> them keep going on and saying, "Hey you, stop it!" Easier to
> stop it *before it gets out of hand.* (emphasis added) (Margaret)

Teaching is reconstructed through this manipulation metaphor
as a kind of performance, which involves "being in touch," "dealing
with," "handling problems." Professional needs are constructed as
akin to the skills of the juggler, even the sleight of hand of the conjurer,
using "tricks of the trade" to perform clever manipulative tasks. This
reworked "teacher" not as *mutual friend* but as *actor* is traditionally
and, in the case of the conjurer, necessarily remote from the audience.
What the actor/conjurer must never do is to communicate the mechanics of the manipulations to onlookers. In the texts, mention is made of

teachers "hav[ing] to know how to be performers"; "outgoing, flamboyant, interesting, and entertaining"; "one of the teachers was a real clown." When this was wedded to the balance that pre-service teachers articulate as a pedagogical goal, the image of teaching as a type of balancing circus act on a high wire or tightrope strongly suggested itself. The vulnerability of the actor in such a "performance" was also alluded to in texts that reacted to the practicum as "expos[ing] a lot of weaknesses"; "what am I doing here?"; "I know nothing"; "you can't get up there not knowing very much." Further, the image of the failed actor was sustained through descriptions of pre-service teachers as "hit with real problems" during the practicum "lesson/performance." I have referred in the previous chapter to Hatton's analysis of pre-service teacher socialization as "technical bricoleurs." Hatton's assessment of the "performance" of a pre-service teacher she observed during the practicum "appear[ing] totally unconnected with any concern to promote learning" (1991, p. 24) lends some support to the appropriateness of the acting analogy.

This manipulative performance metaphor appeared in tandem with other metaphors used to construct the relational roles of the practicum site and the tertiary campus in the teacher education process. The association of "handling" with what can be "grasped" as "touchable" or "real" constructed the "untouchable" or "unreal" by implication as the "nonhandling" experience of tertiary study:

> I think you learn to deal with situations better by actually handling them rather than by reading about them and being told about them. (Margaret)

> Two weeks of prac made a big difference. I would say it was easily the equal of everything else I've done here. Now the actual experience of standing up in front of a class and trying to, you know, actually being a teacher. I mean, that sort of experience is worth its weight in gold to me. (Ken)

Images of relevant learnings as having substance or solidity (e.g., "worth its weight in gold") seemed to be generated out of this binary formulation of "actual/nonactual" experiences in teacher education. What could be more useful to the circus performer on the high wire than a sense of standing on solid ground or of having a large and visible security net? The "practical/actual" was depicted as "a good foundation"; "having heaps and heaps of information"; "something concrete"; "solid grounding"; "solid foundation"; "basics of how to

teach"; "the real thing"; "actual ins and outs of what you're teaching."
The relevant now became the "touchable." University campuses were
constructed, in turn, as places for "gleaning" among educational de-
bris, "picking up things" that might prove useful, rather than making
meaning. For one student, learning about how to teach is understood
through a metaphor of *storage,* with relevant knowledge depicted as
tangible and compartmentalized into organized and accessible
"boxes":

> I've kind of condensed all this into kind of like one thing,
> that's one part of my brain saying and then the next part of
> my brain, another little box, will be all of this and I think even
> next year it will be another little box with something else and
> then probably toward the end of Third Year you'll start to,
> like, amalgamate the boxes, like joining them all together so
> you've got one big box and then you can just dive into that
> box any time you want to grab what you want. (John)

In most texts, it is the practicum that is seen to provide what is
solid, storable, foundational. When the practicum is conflated with the
"practical," "nonpracticum" experiences may be constructed as all of
a piece, to be equated with what is "unreal," "untouchable," "theoretical." By contrast with what is able to be handled, the university's offerings were constructed as light and ephemeral, "sort of very airy-fairy,"
as "background" rather than foreground, "drawn out," "dragged out,"
rather than compact and accessible to the hand. If the work of the
teacher is to be understood as a manipulating/performing act that
requires solid and tangible foundations, then the learner must be
audience/onlooker.

These second-year texts were significant not so much for their
"loss of idealism" as for their construction of students as a particular
sort of *audience,* an audience in need of the therapy of teacher-as-
performer. "Keeping the audience interested in the performance" had
displaced "students-as-coactors." Two-way dialogic metaphors in first-
year texts tended to give way to "providing a good show" in which
the only overtly active role is that of the teacher. While the rhetoric of
"individual differences" was very much still in evidence, texts now
articulated the teaching task as "the need to tell the kids why they
were there, where they were going." (It is in second-year texts that the
descriptor of students as "kids," like the noun "discipline," makes its
first appearance.) Scholarship loses out to conveyancing ability. "It's no
use being brilliant at it if you can't get your message across to the kids";

"unless you can convey it to the students in a way they understand, then you're not a good teacher." The implications for teacher education were that it provide more small, bright, and shiny pedagogical objects:

> Teacher education should also involve learning the content. At the moment we do learn content, but I believe we could be learning more [especially trivial little things that can grab the interest of the kids] content than what we presently do. (Trevor)

"Teacher-as-actor/performer" reconstructs a notion of good teaching as a "talent" that is "natural" and cannot be learned. A "grab-bag" of tricks is a bonus. The texts that speak of people who are "naturally talented," "naturally good," tend to privilege "personality" and "experience" to the virtual exclusion of pedagogical knowledge:

> The institution cannot teach one to be a good teacher. This will rely on a person's enthusiasm . . . I still believe that. I think you can be taught just the basics but it depends on the person and it depends on their own enthusiasm whether they're going to be good or bad. (Rita)

> Some people are just naturally talented. There's one person in my class he says "Right, we've got this assignment" and we'll go to the library and he'll start explaining what he thinks he's done to the same stage as I and he did that last year too. He was just naturally good at explaining and getting everything organized. Which is one of the main things I think in teaching. (Trevor)

This construction of teaching places the practicum at the very heart of the pedagogical process of becoming a teacher, in that it is understood as the only possibility that exists for a "live" performance (teaching) to a "real" audience (students-as-kids). This construction marginalizes university knowledge-building as "worthless" where it is not readily "transferable" through a performance/show that "real" students "stay tuned to":

> I sort of put the Education subjects, you know, philosophy and those sorts of things, and the TS (Teaching Studies) subjects probably on a 50-50 scale. I think you've gotta have the knowledge but the knowledge is no good if you can't get it

across, if you don't know how to get it across. You know, if you can't relate with kids, if they're just going to turn off from you, then you're not achieving anything. Your knowledge is not worth anything. (Margaret)

The role that teacher educators and supervising teachers play in sustaining the metaphor of the active, performing, and naturally talented teacher, and the passively watching, entertained student, through their role as "performance critics," must not be overlooked. The language of *survival*, a theme so much focused on in previous influential studies of the concerns of pre-service teachers (e.g., Fuller, 1969), appears very little in second-year texts. However, when it does, it is, as Beauchamp and Parsons suggest (1989), in the context of supervisor/pre-service teacher power relations:

I still feel that way [idealistic] . . . unless something really dramatic happens this year . . . like failing prac. (Andrea)

It [the need for public speaking] was brought to my attention by my supervising teacher I have. I mean she could see sort of immediately that I hadn't had a lot of practice at that. And it was then that it suddenly occurred to me that it was a disadvantage . . . it [prac] exposed a lot of weaknesses. Strengths? Well, no, not really. (Ken)

Hopefully I'll have nice teachers there and they'll pull me through . . . they just threw me into it and I survived. (Marilyn)

Metaphors of teaching as performance within the potentially dangerous and unnatural medium of water were evident for the first time in these second-year texts. It could be argued that "survival" here, as "keep[ing] your head above water," is more akin to "treading water" than to swimming, a pragmatic rather than a creative endeavor. The notion of the practicum as "the deep end" where pre-service teachers "sink or swim" is pervasive in pre-service needs talk. This metaphor is sustained by students in their depiction of themselves as having "shallow" knowledge, equipping them only for pedagogical shallows, not the "deeper understanding" needed for artistic performance when feet can no longer make contact with the security of the bottom.

One second-year student was much more analytical of the context of power relations rather than presuming a lack in the author's own "performance" skills. She identified relational issues in a way not found in other second-year texts:

> And you're sitting there thinking, "Am I going to pass prac?" and, as a result, you know, you sort of think, well, O. K. so I could turn around and do it like I would like to, or I could do it the way my prac teacher wants me to do it and pass prac. So you did it the way your prac [teacher says], and it does start to make you feel like there's a division between college and prac but . . . that's pretty sad really, I mean, 'cos I think college has the right idea about how teaching should be . . . probably gets easier to get disillusioned once you're out there and you're having to deal with bureaucracies all the time. (Roxanne)

In a minority of texts, including those written and spoken by Roxanne (quoted above), a different set of metaphors was evident. These students used an "open-eye" metaphor to depict a change of consciousness brought about by their course and their prac experience. Students depicted themselves as "woken up" or "seeing . . . in a different light." Their needs talk was much more critical of the "actualities" of prac and much more focused on power struggles in teaching:

> I think a lot of it is, sort of, wake up and see where you are, you know, [laughs] because I mean I never thought I was ignorant but, at the same time, even though I knew what was going on, I didn't really think about the implication. . . . And going out on prac I think also helped. Not because I don't think I got any valuable teaching experience out of it [laughs]. But just the contrast between, sort of, what we were being told here and what was happening in the schools . . . the people in the staffroom would sit there and they were so miserable. . . . And, you know, realizing that sort of teacher out there tends to be the norm rather than the exception is pretty frightening. . . . I think that it is a kind of political issue with me. (Roxanne)

Another student provides a negative anecdote to elaborate on the prac as an "eye opener":

> Prac, prac. [laughs] That was an eye opener, a real eye opener. . . . Well, I went to Mt. Gravatt High and that's quite

a small school and I had the Year Eights. They just didn't
know what was happening. The teacher I had was from the
old school, very behavioristic method ... there was a kid in
there and he was quite, not slow, but my teacher thought he
was stupid first of all ... she brought in an exam paper of his
and we were looking at it, and from the looks of it he looked
dyslexic, and they did not even pick it up we were just like
going, "Woh!" Oh I could have strangled that teacher for not
picking [the possibility of dyslexia] up. (Dee)

These same students described themselves and their views as
"changed." They recognized but did not seek to explain away inconsistencies between first- and second-year texts:

VERA: I think I've learnt so much more over the last year. I
had a different perception of teaching when I first started
than what I do now. I think perhaps that I thought teaching
was, you know, A-B-C-D, and that's what you did, and this is
how you work, whereas now since I've got ... a lot of issues
that I came in with very stagnant ideas on, they've changed,
so I think it's a personal change. That's why it's now more
educating myself ... there's another part where I said students to be able to express themselves fairly yet still within
the constraints of what the Education Department allows. I
don't agree with that anymore.

ERICA: What was it that you don't agree with?

VERA: That students are only able to express themselves to a
certain degree but the Education Department still dictates
what they can sort of really say. I think a student word about
something not being approved of by the Admin, it wouldn't
worry me anymore ... a person weighed up an option instead
of so and so in the office.

Later in the same interview, Vera described the teaching she observed
on prac as a kind of "schizophrenia." She spoke of

seeing teachers in a different light ... that they are human
and once they walk out of the classroom, they become different people. It was funny watching my supervising teacher
become this person, whereas, when we had lunch together,

she was completely different. This is really strange, because you see your teachers at school as being that "front-faced" person.

This subset of second-year texts clearly differed from mainstream exemplars in their construction of teaching, in that they were more focused on "critique" than on "performance." Already, this group has understood their own perspectives as problematic in the teacher education culture. Their privileging of critique over "imitative practice" is now being perceived as a "minority view" irritating to others:

> There is a lot of problem [*sic*] with power relations work and ... there's big problems like the teachers don't have enough control. I mean they're the people who know most about education and they don't have enough say. [When] I think [about] things like that I can get quite verbose [laughs]. You know, people choose to pick an argument with me. (Roxanne)

Those for whom critique is important represent themselves as having changed a great deal and as being open to this experience:

> I've learnt so much more . . . a lot of issues I came in with very stagnant ideas on, they've changed. . . . I think it's a personal change. . . . I hope by this time next year I will have changed a bit again maybe not as drastically maybe. (Vera)

> I do actually, reading back, I think "O God, what have I written!" . . . we are learning how to question and inquire. (Dee)

> I have now learnt that, that knowledge has become a part of me. (Mandy)

For this group, it is student difference as "cultural diversity" rather than as "a range of abilities" or "a range of problems" that appeared to inform the reconstruction of teacher work as the protection of student rights:

> There are so many things that we have to deal with like the fact that there is multiethnic and multicultural people, hugely diverse groups in the schools . . . there are just so many issues out there created by that. (Roxanne)

> It's really important to give every student a right to be there
> in the class. (Mandy)

Further, they were more likely to retain the two-way metaphors evident in their initial texts, or even begin to generate them for the first time:

> It's a two-way thing. It's not just the teacher is the one we go
> to for help. I mean that equally I think that I'll go to my students for help. (Mandy)

> I think having a comfortable relationship is having the students' respect really. I think you can have respect and still
> have a sort of comfort . . . a friendly relationship with the students and that depends on how you want to run your classroom, I suppose. (Roxanne)

> I've changed my ideas about being the big dominator out in
> front of the classroom. . . . I want to learn as much about myself so that I understand me before I [teach]. (Vera)

This subset of texts, in its focus on personal and professional change and its preparedness to critique the pedagogical practices of both the university and the practicum, seemed more characteristic of the type of politicized *oppositional needs talk* that Fraser (1989) identifies in the construction of welfare needs. In them, student voices have not been silenced by the discourses of management or of therapy emanating from either university or the practicum. There was evidence of ongoing personal and professional struggle, which makes their teacher preparation more onerous yet more likely to be rewarding for their future students than those student voices that attempt to echo a cacophony of "expert" supervisory, inspectorial, and teacher voices.

Interestingly, these texts shared with others a critique of an element of the teacher education course that is often perceived as its most "practical" component. The brunt of criticism right across the texts was leveled not at theoretical subjects, as the literature would have it (Carr, 1980), but at those subjects that sought, unsuccessfully according to the student texts, to imitate the "actual." A first-year Teaching Studies subject (TS2900), in which micro-teaching was a central component, was described as "a generally negative experience," "the bludge [do nothing] subject," "too long and drawn out," "five-minute micro-lessons gave us no idea of anything," "didn't seem to have any bearing on teaching." This subject was identified as failing to provide the necessary "link" between university and field experience:

> I just couldn't see like in our TS, that is our subject that links up with prac, so I assumed that we'd be, fair enough we had to do lessons and prepare lessons and things like that, but when we went out to prac, everything that I'd learnt, I'd say, "This is our lesson plan," you know, and they'd say "This isn't how to do it," you know. "This is wrong, this doesn't apply." So I sort of thought well what's the point of being here if I'm not being taught, you know, what's happening outside. (Rosemarie)

What seems noteworthy here is that all university offerings become tainted by the failure of this "technical" and imitative subject to demonstrate its relevance to pre-service teachers in the field. Perhaps what has been understood to be the failure of "theory" may need to be reassessed as a consequence, in part, of the failure of those course elements that do purport to be skill-based, such as micro-teaching, to translate into worthwhile knowledge outside the institution. It is interesting to note that the criticisms leveled at micro-teaching as "fake" are, in some later texts, also leveled at prac teaching. Constructing false models that purport to be "practical" but are "not real situations" is responded to negatively by students.

Oppositional students seemed to take their critique further, as the following illustrate:

> It's no use learning how to run the overhead projector and turn on the video successfully without being laughed at, if you've got nothing meaningful to say about the video or what's on the OHP. (Vera)

> I hated TS last year . . . you don't have to have 15 weeks of lectures on how to turn on a video . . . we hated it. I think the lecturers hated it . . . I suppose it is important to have the technical know-how but I think it's a bit overdone. . . . I don't think that had an awful lot of effect on me at all apart from feeling that I wasn't getting guidance where I felt I needed it. (Roxanne)

These students decentered "technique" from its dominant status in pre-service needs talk, when it was experienced as a disembodied set of skills, peripheral to teacher work rather than at its core.

Only one of the students drew overtly on the specific language of a subject discipline. Despite evidence of particular content being "recycled" through the texts, it was only the discipline of Drama that seemed to have impinged in any demonstrable way on the text itself. John, a Drama student, spoke of the importance of "interpreting class signals," or "how to interpret and re-class the signals," or of "reading their signals":

> You can read the class's signals like different people walking into the classroom which is one of the most important things, like when they're coming in you just, especially for drama, you go, "O, the class." You can see some people are high energy and some people are low energy and some people . . . in between. So you read them and then you've got to think of something that will bring them all to the same energy level. That's reading the signals, but with problem students and all that, it's harder to respond to them. . . . Like when they're down the back mucking around, you've got to think . . . they're probably at the high energy level so you've got to think of something high but maybe to bring them lower, so you've got to think of other activities like that.

Much of John's needs talk appeared to be focused on "problem students down the back mucking around." It was in second year through the oral interview that the role played by John's own personal biography was first understood as important in constructing teaching this way:

> I've probably been a disruptive person in class too and just sat down the back and mucked around and didn't know much about teaching in general.
>
> You've had teachers that have been all authoritative and just knock you down and everything. All they want is work, work, work, and you go, "I will never be like that," and you think well maybe if I go through the whole system I will turn out like that. There will be none of this left, and I just say, depends on the type of teacher, I know that I will always be able to communicate and respond with the students and try to get on.

Later, however, John provided quite a violent metaphor that seems to be a good reason for contradicting his declaration of "never being like that":

> You have the attitude that all students are good, then you're going to get hammered to pieces because you're gonna have these students down the back like I did and they're just going off and doing their own thing and you hear, Oh no, I haven't learnt on management. Maybe I should just try something that the prac teachers, my guiding teacher's done. "Just stand at the back please," and I'll be authoritative about [it]. "Stand at the back or just shut-up and listen!"

It was not only in this case that personal biography overtly informed reconstructions of teacher's work in texts. In the interviews conducted in the second year, during which students reflected on their texts, students provided a number of anecdotes to explain the presence of particular needs talk expressed in their own written texts. Mandy elaborated her denunciation of "favoritism" in the first-year text:

> I remember emphasizing this favoritism bit 'cos I'd just come back from my trip overseas to the Royal Ballet School where it was totally like that . . . on the other hand I know how it feels to be the favorite because, when I was going through high school and in my drama subjects, "Oh, pick Mandy, pick Mandy," all the time, the first person that'd do everything, and it just leaves everyone else feeling "Well, what am I here for?" It's just not good and when I was in my classes over at the Royal Ballet School I really thought about teaching. I felt like getting up to my dance teacher and saying, "Alright, you might know dance and ballet, mate, but you sure as hell don't know how to conduct a class and how to make people feel good about being here." Yeah, so that's basically where it all stemmed from.

Another student, Melanie, elaborated on the inclusion of the secondary teacher's need of an "air of mystery" in her first-year text, an inclusion that she now felt was no longer appropriate to her needs talk:

> That came from personal experience I had of a teacher at school who got to know everyone too well and everyone got to know him and, sort of people, he went to parties with stu-

dents and he was a really nice guy but he was just not a good teacher in the classroom because people couldn't, he couldn't draw that line between sort of being out of the classroom and in the middle of the classroom. I suppose coming straight from school that's what I was thinking but it sort of disappeared, didn't it? I think to me now it's more important getting to know the kids and their getting to know you.

Yet her "change of heart" in second year, evident in her stressing the need to know "a great deal about the students which [sic] they are teaching," appears to be founded on another particular experience of student/teacher relations, this time during the practicum:

> There was this kid in Grade 7 class and before I even saw the class, the teacher warned me about him and said, "He's a real mongrel and will bash girls up and will back-chat and will rave on and on and on," and he did everything the teacher said he'd do. And the teacher sort of explained like everyone thought that this kid had been, you know, abused at home by his parents, which, when I first thought about it, I thought this one kid I'm just gonna forget all about him, but when he explained to me why, I sort of went out of my way to help him, and we got to the stage, you know I was only there for a week, but, by the end of the week, we could talk. I mean he wouldn't abuse me and back-chat like he did at the beginning of the week, which made me feel good that I, but if I hadn't known that was the cause of all his problems, I probably would have thought, "You mongrel kid, get away!" but making a bit of an effort, you know made a big difference.

Following this experience, her needs talk was much more inclusive of and responsive to context:

> Teachers should also have an understanding of the community in which the school operates, the resources available within the community [or not available] and any possible difficulties unique to the community.

For Melanie, studies of context that had been part of her Education Studies foundational units in first year were all the more meaningful as a result:

The education subjects we did back then, I really enjoyed them and found both of them very helpful. There's something I mentioned too about the community—that assignment we did—I sort of found that very useful and some of the things in there that I hadn't thought about before, you know, where the school is situated and the community that it's in . . . I became aware of some of those things.

A cycle of meaning-making seemed to have been created for Melanie when an experience of being involved in a positive way during the practicum "makes sense" of "college theory." Her text, in turn, did not reconstruct the teacher education process as a binary system of "theory *or* practice," but rather spoke of the "practical" as inclusive of some pedagogical ideas often understood as "theoretical."

The most dramatic change in needs talk occurred in the texts written and spoken by Ken. While his first-year talk expresses the need to "know how to encourage learning rather than to teach parrot fashion, how to teach from a positive point of view . . . to encourage not discourage," his second-year talk is highly focused on "standing in front of a class . . . public speaking." The practicum for him is "worth its weight in gold" in that it was "a bit of a shock," "expos[ing] a lot of weaknesses" through a supervising teacher who was "pretty hard," "giving me a little kick along all the time." When elaborating on his own understanding of teaching after the practicum, Ken's response was now markedly different from that of first year:

I mean whatever you do, you've got a class to handle. Whatever else happens. You've got to get them in there, get them to sit down, basically get them, you know, to listen to what you're saying or doing, or, you know, take instructions in as to what you want them to say or do. So, yeah, I'm talking about gaining the experience.

When asked to elaborate on the apparent contradictions of the two written texts, he made the following oral response:

I suppose I mean you can be practical and idealistic, I suppose, but I think in this second one I've got a much better idea of what the teaching actually involves. I think most of that probably came from prac.

For Ken, the great value of the prac ("worth its weight in gold") appeared to be the extent to which he felt inadequate, as distinct from university, where he felt competent.[2]

The unusual extent to which Ken seemed to equate the value of an experience with the extent to which he perceived himself to fail suggested to me that Ken's "commonsense" images of himself were about appropriate failure rather than unlikely success. It was as though the prac had "got it right" in assessing him as "performing" poorly. A mature student on entry (29 years old), Ken had already had experiences of education and of work and nonwork that were important in his own construction of himself in this way:

> I just felt as though it [university] was an alien world that I didn't understand, and I mean, doctors' and dentists' kids went to those places, and, you know, kids that are the sons of truck-drivers, you know, buy trucks. To me school didn't have a lot to do with where you ended up. . . .
>
> Well, for the first 12 months after I left school I had trouble getting a job but then I got one about 18 months later, stayed there for 6 years. That gave me money in the bank, a bit of security, bought a car so I could get around in. I bought some real estate, you know, sort of got some security behind me, you know. Well then, the company went bankrupt, that sort of left me with nothing to do I suppose. Then I sort of thought, you know, I didn't want to go back to the same thing. I mean I liked that company but the idea of starting from the ground again. . . . You know, I'd rather be out of work. So for me it was a case of, you know, do I sit here and be out of work for the rest of my life, or do I, you know. . . .
>
> I'd already started at night school. You know, 'cos I could see the writing on the wall so I enrolled at night school to keep moving. And I did two years there to re-do my Senior. . . .
>
> I did not want to be a drain on anybody. . . .
>
> My father is a truck-driver. He hasn't got money to spare. So that was pretty crucial too, you know. . . . Some colleges only aimed at the private school sector but the kids are actually allocated a school the entire time they're there. I think it's one day a week that they're at that school and they teach in front of that class. That rather appeals to me because when you can actually learn the kids' names, and, I mean, your supervising teacher will be marking you for the whole year,

I imagine, I mean I'm not sure on all the details but they could see your improvement and, I mean, they could see how you're doing, give you the tips. . . .

The image of teacher as performer/manipulator was even more strongly maintained by Ken in the needs talk he generated in his third and final year (e.g., "how to project," "I believe good teachers would make good actors," "they must literally act out the role of a teacher and change their personality to suit the role they must play"). Could it be that the actor as "disguise" or as a "covering up" of the person had become, rather tragically, an indispensable notion in this case?

THIRD-YEAR STORIES

While Ken and, to a lesser extent, Trevor maintained and even augmented the metaphor of teaching as theatrical performance in the texts they produced in their third and last year of professional preparation, a "third" generation of metaphors generated different constructions of teaching and teacher needs in many of the other texts produced. By third year, this group of pre-service teachers had experienced a full extended and "inspected" practicum, where they had been required to do less observation and more teaching. They had been assessed on their teaching "performance" in the previous year and were facing another even longer experience of prac teaching at the end of the first semester.

Again, managerial/therapy discourse informed the language of the texts, but they now appeared to reconstruct teacher as "trade worker" in the "industrial setting" of the school. No longer magical conjurer or "trick performer," the teacher was relocated "backstage." With props to be generated and drama to be set in motion, the "teacher-as-stage-manager" was working in a much less glamorous and more constantly demanding world than "teacher-as-actor." The classroom/theater was now a more mundane workplace, with all the bricolage of the industrial site. The students were no longer "audience" but "crew," for whom work must be organized in order for the pedagogical show to go on.

Metaphors of knowledge as "equip[ing] us," of "the mechanics" of teaching, of "using the materials and resources," of "delivering knowledge," of schools as "working environments," of "understanding the working of a classroom," all were suggestive of a *re*presentation of teaching as *industrial* or *trade* work. These metaphors were present not only in texts written at the beginning of third year, but also in the two pieces of text written after the last major practicum at the start of their final semester. The notion of the "experienced" tradesperson as necessarily producing work superior to that of the "apprentice" still learning the trade was strongly implied:

> There is one need for teachers that hasn't really changed over the last few years and that is experience. Both teacher related and life experience. This experience is the building block on which teachers can go forth from [*sic*]. (Trevor)

> Teaching should be learnt through experiential tasks in an apprenticeship or 2 days Uni, 3 days school. Six weeks all at once, once a year is of no benefit to us or the classes we invade for that period of time. (Rosemarie).

> Now I am also thinking of myself as a functioning teacher, than just as a student-teacher, and therefore closer to home, I have needs relating to better teaching strategies, classroom management and an increased understanding of what I am supposed to be doing next year! (Marilyn)

Peter's determination to move "behind the scenes" in the role of teacher as "stage manager" was evident:

> I have continued with the theme of knowing more about what happens behind the scenes or the administrative duties than the actual physical act of teaching. There is a good deal less emphasis on knowing my content areas and a realization that knowledge can be continually acquired. The "art" of teaching has now become the "mechanics" of teaching.

Perhaps the move from "front" to "back" stage has to do not only with the experience of preparing and planning teaching/learning experiences in classrooms during the practicum, but also an experience of having failed "out front." The language of failed performance, the theatrical "flop," made its appearance in third-year texts:

> Having a flop doesn't mean you are a failure as a teacher. I really learnt this on my last [third] prac. I feel that prac makes you feel you have to have this brilliant lesson every lesson, so in this sense it is not realistic. (Vera)

An understanding of "practicum/performance" requirements as un-realistic, as "fake," is evident in Marilyn's text also:

> Prac-teaching sessions are well and good for opening the eyes and giving us some experience but to what extent does it pre-pare us to be the only teacher in the room with your own class [right from the beginning]? It doesn't. It's fake!!

Texts now had the appearance of disjointed fragments of infor-mation, shopping lists or notes rather than coherent paragraphs, and filled with the "bric-a-brac" of what are held to be the "day-to-day realities" of teaching as work. They spoke of "assessment," "marking," "budgeting," "organizing excursions," "resources," "latest develop-ments," "syllabus," "work programs," "computer use," "how to man-age and mediate this working environment," "changes in curriculum," "overhead transparencies." It was almost as though, in their hurry to acquire this "working" knowledge to engage with teacher work as bri-coleurs (Hatton, 1991, p. 127), they had no time to fashion ideas into sentences. The short sharp stabs of a nesting bird at bright and shiny "knowledge objects" as potentially useful in "building their pedagogi-cal nests" next year were evoked here. Indeed, some texts spoke of the importance of "comfort" as an outcome of this stage of frenzied "nest-building":

> Teachers require to know their own individual needs to be able to feel comfortable in teaching their desired subjects. (John)

> It is easier to think about those things I don't feel comfortable about, but these will only come with practice (I hope!). (Peter)

While the focus was still relatively self-centered ("what I'll be do-ing to and for the students" rather than "what the students will be doing for themselves"), there was evidence that some connections were being made about the teacher's role in overseeing student work. The construction of students as "crew," to be provided with work and to be assessed as to its quality, was apparent in embryonic form here. Needs talk now included "how to write exams, written assignments"; "how to design work programs"; "how to organize units of work that is [sic] acceptable"; "how to assess students' achievements effectively and fairly"; "[how to] learn about testing and marking assignments." This positioned the school student as the one for whom tasks are designed and monitored. Yet again, a language of surveillance regulated by managerial discourse was tempered with, or balanced by, an ever-present "therapeutic" talk, in this instance in the form of calls for "counseling/communication skills"; "personalized courses in communication, counseling, human relations and sexuality"; "individualizing learning"; "course aimed at helping teachers to identify specific learning difficulties"; "how to overcome the many disabilities [of] students." Pupils were not merely "crew" but a "problematic crew," whose problems needed to be "coped with," "catered to," "dealt with," by an "expert" or "skilled" counselor/therapist. In the following passage, Rita alluded to the role of the pre-service course itself in the rearticulation of the potentially oppositional language of the student/teacher into an embryonic form of expert needs talk reminiscent of Fraser's (1989) categorization of the same:

> I think that on the one hand, my understanding of my needs as a teacher hasn't changed dramatically in that I'm still big on the counseling/communication skills for teachers. My needs have changed [it seems] in regard to the issue of special ed. This could be because in a Psych. lecture, I concentrated my learning of [*sic*] teaching exceptional students. I don't think it makes me an expert, but maybe I feel I have a very small basic idea on teaching exceptional kids, and at least I know that there are experts [both in human resources and literary] that I could utilize if/when I find myself in this situation.

I was reminded of Fraser's concerns about the potential of "expert needs talk" to redefine people as "cases," and the extent to which this can render individuals passive recipients of therapeutic services. Fraser speaks of the potential of such discourse to become normalizing, aimed at "reforming" or more often stigmatizing "deviancy" (1989, p. 174). The issue is not one of motive, but rather of the process of recuperation of the very best of motives into a form of discourse that has a great deal of potential to depoliticize educational language, and, in turn, deny the political nature of the act of educating itself. The place of a psychologized language of "worker therapy" is very well cemented in our postindustrial work culture. The continuing growth in demand for psychologists in the workplace is a documented feature of current western employment trends.[3] In the construction of teacher as "industrial overseer/stage manager," the image of "teacher-as-counselor" is not juxtaposed against, but already well integrated with, the managerial face of industry. The concerns Bartlett (1991) expresses about the reductionist potential of an industrial model of teaching are not alleviated but are exacerbated by the inclusion of a language of social pathology.

It is important to stress yet again that this metaphorical movement from *mutual friend* in first year, to *actor/performer* in second year, to *stage-manager/industrial overseer* in third year was by no means a universal feature of the texts. The authors of texts that appeared to have retained an oppositional voice, articulated through a more political language of critique in second year, continued to refine and develop a language of critique that resisted both teacher-as-actor and teacher-as-industrial/stage-manager metaphors.

Over the duration of the data collection, some vocabularies appeared to be increasingly informed by a language of social critique. Two students reiterated even more vociferously their ongoing commitment to teacher-as-mutual-friend (Dee and Mandy). In Mandy's case, this is evident in the use of capitals and exclamation marks for emphatic (amplifying?) effect:

> I feel that I have only started to "learn" now! . . . I now value the ability to be able to get my students to really THINK about who they are . . . and about the WORLD and all it involves. I now feel it is vitally important to allow my students the freedom to become SOCIALLY & CRITICALLY AWARE and to THINK.

Dee's text was much less ebullient, more like a dogged determination born of pessimism than delight in the prospect of teaching for change:

> Over the three years of my course I've become less optimistic with the idea of my teaching. . . . I felt I could actually make a difference to the students and the system. I felt I could change and inspire students' lives. . . . Being a history teacher, I was and am concerned with being a resource-based facilitator of learning. My needs have changed from being self-orientated to being class and student orientated. They [needs] have become less idealistic and more practical. I think I've had a crash landing from cloud nine.

It is interesting to note that the move from self- to student focus was understood by the writer here as "practical," rather than "humanistic" or "idealistic."

In texts written by Roxanne and Vera, teacher-as-mutual-friend was now implicit rather than explicit. Texts focused on the contexts in which learning would or would not occur. These two pre-service teachers wrote about the nature of teacher work as mediated by schools with particular configurations of power relations. Theirs was much more a concern to define and explore the contexts with which they would shape their identities as teachers, and how they might inform these contexts. An example of this contextualizing language was provided in Roxanne's elaboration of her changing understanding of her needs:

> To sum it up simply, I think my basic need was [and still is] to understand my role as a teacher. Initially, I didn't really see that role as little more than one of imparting information and, while I was concerned about how that would be done, it was only within a very limited scope. As I studied, I became aware of further dimensions to that role, and, thus, my direct needs changed—for example at the beginning of second year I was particularly concerned with the needs of the students as learners and how I could fulfil those needs and I wanted to learn things that would assist me in those areas. By third year I had refocused and I was most concerned about knowing things which would give me power—on one level knowing and feeling confident about your role as a teacher and on another level knowledge of the problems etc. I was likely to face in schools so that I would be prepared to overcome them.
> My needs have really changed as I've better understood how the system works and how I will fit into that system. Most of the things I believed on the first day I still believe but I have reordered my priorities. As I see it, teaching is very much political. It's not so much that content and technique etc have taken a back seat to politics but rather that they are, I think, political issues. I certainly didn't realize that in first year, and the worst thing is, when I realized it, the realization really undermined my confidence (At the beginning of second year I was pretty confident). I'm glad it's happened now rather than next year though.

Vera added to this representation of teaching as "very much political" a critique of her own teacher education institution and its "products," and an awareness of herself as a minority voice:

My needs as a teacher still haven't been met at this institution, while I am ready to go out to the "real world" and teach. This course hasn't covered a lot of areas that I would expect a teaching course to cover. I did not recognize these additional areas when I first came, I attribute this to the fact I came in as one of the white middle-class masses and I am leaving as one of the aware minorities. I still feel that many students at this institution havn't [*sic*] changed any of their ideas and it's an awful thing to say, but some of them I would hate teaching my children.

Vera found fault with the failure of the institution to "teach us how the profession works." Interestingly, she uses the metaphor of a religious order in her attempt to represent the "walled-off" relationship between university and schools:

College is too much of a cloistered environment. . . . It seems to me that all the teachers who want to change the system end up lecturing. A person who has ideas about change within those four walls [classroom] is working against such a brick wall, not only with fellow associates/workers but with students.

Roxanne also speaks of a world of "harsh reality" waiting "outside," and its potential to cause her to lose her ideals. She claimed to need

self-knowledge as well as knowledge of what's "out there". . . . my biggest fear is that in the harsh reality of the system . . . all my ideals will be lost. I'm fairly sure of what I believe about teaching and what I'd like to do but what I've seen of the school system scares me. All the people who appear to believe what I do seem to leave. What could I be taught here to overcome this fear?

This final poignant question throws down the gauntlet to all involved in the initial teacher education project, including critical teacher educators. It is not enough to send teachers out with "raised critical consciousness" without addressing the "political" issues of content and technique. Simon's (1988) call for teachers to "guard against hopelessness" (p. 4) seems to be all the more urgent for pre-service teachers, who are armed with little more than awareness of social injustice and good intentions. While Simon, like so many other avant-garde writers, is able to pose the question and to make the critique, he too is silent on the matter of strategies that might help in addressing this fear. Could it be that, in our haste to critique reductionist formulae for teaching, avant-garde educators have offered little more than cautionary tales when it comes to issues of actually doing it? Has critical teacher education discourse conflated the bogeys of technicism with the benefits of sound technique?

Cynicism about university offerings was not confined, in third-year texts, to those I have characterized as "oppositional." It was clear that, by third year, this group of pre-service teachers was at best hopeful and at worst very negative about the value of the preparation their final year was likely to provide. While oppositional texts were critical of "not enough theory to equip us," the "superficial" nature of "practical experience," other critiques were focused on the need for "filling in" knowledge gaps and the fact that this was unlikely to occur at "college." Some examples of how the sentence "I expect what I will be learning here will be . . ." was concluded, which are illustrative of this, are provided below:

> not enough for me to feel confident in my first year of teaching. (Margaret)

> more of the same subjects as in first year with different names or course codes to give us theory in c/room situations, but never offering practical sides of how to implement this in the classroom. (John)

> I expected to learn content, skills, etc. about my own teaching areas, but I also expected to learn other content areas. This "Uni" has failed in its organization of doing this. (Trevor)

At the commencement of the final semester, the theme of the need for "relevance" was augmented by a proliferation of "trade" metaphors of "tying up loose ends," "polishing up . . . weaknesses," or "round[ing] off and fill[ing] in gaps of knowledge." Again, deference to the experience of the tradesperson over the novice is evident, in explaining a perceived lack of skill:

> I firmly believe I need to spend more time in front of a class before I would feel happy about teaching full time in a high school. . . . I still believe that confidence comes from experience, and as I have been consistently told that it is lack of confidence that is hindering my teaching, I believe that it is more experience that I need. (Ken)

Experience is essential in making. . . changes possible. Experiences from teaching, from interacting with various people, from participating in different roles, etc. can help build this experience needed to adapt and act. (Trevor)

A feature that seemed to distinguish oppositional or defiant voices in these texts was the "prac as real/prac as fake" distinction. Roxanne's "version" of the practicum contrasted markedly with that of Trevor, informed as it was by "gaining experience":

Sometimes a tertiary education is about as useful as a kick in the bum, which means that all prac [for pre-service training] would probably be more beneficial. (Trevor)

The lack comes from the feeling that . . . prac . . . bears no relation to what teaching is actually like—it's so artificial, as one of the teachers said to me, student teachers aren't "real people"—so everything that takes place on prac is slightly false. (Roxanne)

What Roxanne did believe prac provided her, however, was a taste of the power relations that would characterize her early experience of teaching:

I think when we get out there the relationships we have with the staff is going to be like our experience on prac in that some teachers will be supportive but the majority will either ignore us, or resent us—at the very least we'll be the lowest rung on the ladder and after my experience on prac I'm not looking forward to that!

As a postscript to the pre-service teachers whose biographies appeared to strongly inform their texts early in their course, the responses of John, Mandy, Melanie, and Ken to third-year writing tasks were interesting.

John, once a self-described "disruptive person in class," now perceived himself to have been "disciplined" to pursuing "a new direction" in which "classroom management is becoming the dominant factor":

Over the past few years my needs have changed from being the young, inexperienced almost naive to the matter of fact and semi-professional disciplined teacher of [*sic*] a result of experiencing a diverse variety of teaching situations. When I began my college education I seemed to focus on the importance of communication with students and requiring the methods of teaching to accomplish that goal. The following year finds a new direction whereby "classroom management" is becoming the dominant factor. The last being my own identity to teach effectively and convincingly. The reasons behind these changes may lie in my prac experience by which I learned where my weaknesses lie and where my professional growth will occur.

For Mandy, the earlier theme of avoiding favoritism had completely disappeared in favor of an enthusiasm for and a confidence in teaching as "guiding them to educate themselves." In the wake of a life centered on performance, her text was itself an on-going communicative "performance," embellished by punctuation, capitals, underlines, and so on:

> I hope to increase my abilities to give students situations . . . whereby they can explore existing social issues. I want my students to be THINKERS. . . . I am very confident in my ability and quality of communication. I think I am an excellent communicator in terms of understanding *WHAT* is being communicated and *HOW* it is being received [feelings etc.].
> I want to learn through trial and error exactly what teaching is all about and what I WANT IT TO BE ALL ABOUT. . . . I think there will be a marked difference between the two! I hope to have the ability to give my students the opportunity to be able to be EDUCATED!

Her text also provided examples of the subject-discipline language identified in John's second-year text. Like John, Mandy is a Drama teacher:

> [Secondary teachers need to know] how to communicate HONESTLY! how to read signals/verbal/nonverbal and act in accordance to [*sic*] those signals.

Melanie appeared to have stayed with her theme of the nature of the student-teacher relationship. However, it would seem that, in part, she returned to her earlier "air of mystery" language, which she temporarily deserted in second year. Her understanding of teachers as "not becoming too familiar/friendly" in third-year texts was elaborated as a sort of "midway" point, a "balance" between first- and second-year constructions:

> I still feel that teachers need an understanding of adolescents and that process is more important than content. One of the areas where I feel I may have changed my understanding is in the area of student-teacher relationships. Having had a Grade 10 Class on Prac that I developed an excellant [*sic*] relationship with, I now greatly appreciate the need to have students accept you as a teacher before they accept you for your "good mate" qualities.

Ken was still very much focused on teaching as an exposing of weaknesses, and therefore a teacher education program as "support." For him, "an increasing amount of time in the classroom" was understood to be the solution, with the proviso that

> this time would be spent with someone who has already seen me teach, who knows my strengths and weaknesses and who could give me help and assistance accordingly.

The performance metaphor was strongly maintained through insistence on teachers' knowing "how to project themselves." He spoke of a "required image" as "that of a person with confidence and authority." He still hoped, during this third year, to learn "how to handle a class [discipline]"; he still saw the ideal learning experience for him as "in front of a real class of 20 or 30 adolescent teenagers."

A NEW TALE OF SOCIALIZATION

As a researcher, I can tell a new tale out of this sort of data—one that reinvents the socialization of pre-service teachers in initial teacher education. It has already been stated that the purpose of this type of narrative is not to "disprove" time-honored understandings of the process whereby teachers acquire their professional perspectives. Rather, it attempts to rearticulate how pre-service teacher education informs this socialization, through inquiry into the complexity and diversity of the ways that prospective teachers "write" and "rewrite" themselves in the texts they generate about their own needs.

Commonly held views of pre-service teacher education as either a *liberalizing* experience "washed out" by school experience (Hoy & Rees, 1977; Morrison & MacIntyre, 1969) or as *conservative* in its effects (Ginsburg, 1988; Gordon, 1985; Hatton, 1991; Zeichner & Tabachnick, 1981) tend to construct the pre-service experience as all of a piece, as though "understanding otherwise" was not possible for individuals whose own discursive practices are shaped by a monolithic dominant discursive tradition. What the above analysis reveals is the possibility for either or neither scenario, given the dynamic and complex nature of the interplay of the *contexts* of teacher education. While there is no doubting the power of the practicum as a "watershed" experience, it does not always "collapse" a potentially progressive political agenda. Neither the depoliticization of potentially oppositional talk nor, alternatively, its repoliticization into a "discourse of resistance" is a foregone conclusion.

The openness of student language to a variety of discursive reconstructions of teaching must not be forgotten by critical teacher educators who can be frustrated by pre-service teachers' "struggle for pedagogies" (Gore, 1993). It is otherwise too tempting to force-feed them on social justice through an evangelical language of critique.

What seems to me to be more useful in terms of developing a language of possibility is to provide the conditions for a mutual examination of the many inconsistencies and contradictions in versions of teacher work generated over time and from one individual to another. Roxanne and Ken, for example, seemed to enter with very similar views about the nature of teacher work. Yet their oral and written texts change over time in ways that are very dissimilar in their metaphorical construction and focus. Why is Roxanne's oppositional voice amplified and Ken's apparently silenced by a program that is, at least superficially, the same? What role is played by biography here? And what role is the result of particular relationships with particular lecturers and particular subject areas? Or of particular school settings? Can we speak of "stages" of resistance that can be identified as "embryonic" or "adult" oppositional talk? How do avant-garde educators respond to the notion that the "politics of technique" is a matter on which they have been deemed by avant-garde students as inappropriately silent?

At the very least, this analysis moves us on to contemplate a different set of questions rather than to continue to debate the liberal or conservative effects of the pre-service experience, or to rue the lack of opportunity for liberating pedagogy at the pre-service level. The binaries that we have invented for telling our tales about teacher preparation are not as *telling* as we have held them to be. It is through different accounts of our own and our students' discourse shaped by the power relations of the pre-service experience that we should now seek to achieve mutually beneficial social and pedagogical arrangements.

What this analysis challenges is the belief that teacher preparation ought to be dismissed as relatively inconsequential when compared with the power of other biographical experiences to inform the teacher socialization process (Grant & Sleeter, 1985; Hogben & Lawson, 1983; Lortie, 1975). If new metaphors are at the heart of new theories, then it could well be argued that a great number of new theories are being generated by pre-service teachers over this time. The rewriting of teacher-as-mutual-friend through the metaphorical construction of teacher-as-actor/performer and its reconstruction, teacher-as-industrial-overseer/stage-manager, is a recurring pattern across a number of the texts analyzed here. Further, there is evidence of very different processes producing other constructions of teaching, including the notion that it is a political endeavor, and that students speak of themselves as "changing" in accordance with these new imperatives.

Of course, this narrative cannot predict whether these metaphors will continue to inform the professional work of these particular teachers in the future. It does, however, provide reason to be cautious in dismissing initial teacher education as discursively "uneventful," just as it sounds a note of warning about labeling it simply conservative or liberal.

I would conclude from my own analysis that there is little cause for optimism or for complacency as to the ease with which progressive pedagogical practice is likely to be learned in initial teacher education processes. The power of entrenched discursive traditions to serve a hegemonic function through depoliticizing potentially oppositional vocabularies is very much in evidence in these pre-service texts. This is not simply manifested in a language of "custodialism," "managerialism" as the symptom of "pupil control ideology," but is the effect of its symbiosis with an apparently gentler, more innocuous language of therapy that reconstructs future students as "suitable cases for treatment." It is the power of these discursive fragments to act symbiotically, as a complementary couplet maintaining "the right balance" of idealism and realism or humanism and custodialism, that needs probing. The regulative effects of these discourses give apparent coherence to instrumentalist images of teaching in a way that avant-garde traditions of critique seem unable to do.

Reconstruction of the stories that have been told about teacher socialization requires examination of the interplay of these images, rather than continuing to speak of them as opposite ends of a discursive continuum. Further, these effects must be explored in the context of the psychology of particular individuals and locations. The small and precarious tales we generate from such work are more likely than our "definitive studies" to inform us as individuals about the successes, struggles, and setbacks we experience in our own daily work with pre-service teachers.

Avant-garde educators now have the mechanisms by which to incorporate complementary languages of "construct" into languages of critique, in order to more successfully challenge those texts perceived to be functioning hegemonically. The language of student idealism can be a useful language for a progressive pedagogy. Yet it also contains much that can be easily recuperated to serve instrumentalist ends, since student texts as oppositional talk continue to accommodate and resist in a range of ways the expert talk of educational institutions. The challenge for progressive teacher educators is to bring these very processes and the local conditions in which they occur forward for scrutiny. And this must mean subjecting our own teaching and research practices to the sorts of critiques we are adept at making of the work of others.

In the chapter that follows, I indicate how this research tale was of pedagogical use to me and the research participants in their final semester of formal teacher preparation, by allowing us to reflect collectively on the partiality and precariousness of the individual stories of lecturer and students alike.

CHAPTER 5

QUESTIONING THE FACT
Advocacy in Initial Teacher Education Research

TAKING RISKS

The tales told in preceding chapters are all produced, at least to some extent, out of my frustration with the traditions that have informed ways of writing teacher education. For me, the source of this frustration has been the way in which initial teacher education research writing continues to congeal into either/or and from/to binary formulations to explain complex, incoherent, and contradictory practices. Calls for educational research that copes with complexity are, of course, not new. Indeed, the failure of teacher education research to "tap the complexities and dynamics of the everyday experiences" of the novice (Battersby, 1986, p. 4) and the need to break new ground in pre-service research (Atkinson & Delamont, 1985; Beyer & Zeichner, 1981; Ginsberg & Newman, 1981; Popkewitz, 1979) have been familiar themes in over a decade of teacher education writing. Atkinson and Delamont's (1985) claim that researchers "seem to have become shackled by the chains of their parent theories" (p. 78) seems no less true now than it was over a decade ago. So debates continue in teacher education literature as to whether the pre-service "experience," conceptualized as a monolith, is essentially liberal or conservative, whether we need less theory and more practice, whether students are too idealistic or too custodial, whether we now need more studies that are quantitative rather than qualitative, and so on.

The assumption on which much of the research and the debate are based is that one set of language practices is adequate to new research, and that one research model will best serve any one particular project. Despite work that challenges positivist assumptions about validity in educational research methodology (e.g., Lather, 1991a, 1993), there are only a few tentative signs of a movement to take advantage of the way contemporary debates might generate more eclecticism within individual studies. "Legitimate" research is still conceived of as staying within one particular paradigm, rather than involving risky (invalid?) experimentation across, and even beyond, traditional paradigms and research languages. Tisher and Wideen's conclusions, in an assessment of the past decade of teacher education research worldwide, are depressing testimony to this methodological conservatism and the resultant impoverishment of the tales constructed out of teacher education research:

> We see a disconcerting set of studies with no coherent objectives and a lack of balance; poor anchoring to the practical, day-to-day problems in teacher education; a pre-dominance of surveys with minimal experimentation on new ways of delivering teacher education; unwarranted overkill with sophisticated statistical analyses; studies designed and driven by persons who are often not involved in educating teachers; little or no compelling effect on policy or practice . . . in a number of cases, projects of dubious rigour. Researchers appear to pursue their own interests . . . investigatory samples draw on captive groups of teacher trainees with no relevant theoretical frameworks serving as substantive scaffolding for studies. The adjectives "exciting", "stimulating", "barrier-breaking", "trend-setting", "knowledge-expanding", and "innovative" can hardly be used to describe research of this nature. (1990, p. 256)

It is no wonder, then, that contemporary critiques of teacher education leave the reader with such a strong sense of déjà vu. For all that has become theoretically possible, there is little evidence of challenging new vistas for teacher education research practices.

PARTICIPATING IN "PRACTICAL" RESEARCH

It must be acknowledged, nevertheless, that participatory educational models now have a much more established place in educational research, as a result of their struggle against scientism and their success in responding to legitimate criticisms of their openness to subjectivism and relativism (McTaggart, 1991b; Wallace, 1987). For more than 50 years, scholars have been noting both the unique opportunities that exist for teachers to be their own researchers, and the potential of participatory research to inform the "theory/practice" nexus in teacher education. From Buckingham's (1926) early exhortations, through Lewin's (1946) and Corey's (1953) experimental models, to the emancipatory "Deakin view" (Carr & Kemmis, 1986; Kemmis & McTaggart, 1988; McTaggart, 1991a), the call for teachers to intervene in their own practices has been an insistent, if historically marginalized, voice in educational inquiry.

The part played by feminists in informing educational research of this type is a crucial one. In seeking to "give voice to the experiences of women usually unheard in theories of learning" (Lather, 1991a, p. 28), feminists have shunned the more rarefied atmosphere of traditional data generation and analysis in favor of an approach that is much more focused on daily realities. Their refusal to proceed from binary distinctions such as theory/practice in education (Yates, 1990) has paved the way for much more dynamic understandings of educational processes than previous modes of inquiry, including action research, have allowed. For feminists, feminism itself is not understood as a "theory," but is embedded in and coalesces with practice, a dimension that gives feminist work much more potential to deal in everyday practices than the "imagined future" of other social critics.

In a domain such as teacher education, where the theory/practice rift has been identified as "a public source of embarrassment" (Hogan, 1988, p. 187), there is much to be learned from such a perspective. Further, Tisher and Wideen's (1990) portrayal of "captive groups of teacher trainees," quoted above, indicates that the issue of outsider/insider relations, while being addressed to some extent in research with practicing teachers, is not being attended to in teacher education at the pre-service level. These two problems are related, inasmuch as human beings are shaped necessarily by the traditions of practice they participate in (Elliot, 1988, p. 164). While teacher educators as researchers tend "to work in the interests of researchers," constructing knowledge "against the interests of those who are [their] clients" (Tripp, 1990, p. 63), it is small wonder that the "academic" knowledge produced out of such research is identified by teachers and potential teachers as both separate from, and irrelevant to, their daily work.

It is true that there have been genuine attempts to remediate this situation with respect to practicing teachers in the last decade. Practicing teachers are being recognized, appreciated, and respected through action research and other dialogic models of inquiry (e.g., Barrow, 1984; Bennison, Jungck, Kantor, & Marshall, 1989). However, it would appear that participatory projects going by the name of action research have, in general, been conducted only with those already in the field. Pre-service teachers have not been understood as appropriate candidates for such studies, because they are not currently "acting" in the professional sense of full-time teaching. The traditional experience of pre-service has ensured that "trainees" remain passive recipients of the "expertise" of others.

Given that practical consciousness is dynamic, or, in Gadamer's (1975) terms, that "the truth of experience always contains an orientation towards new experience" (p. 391), traditions that are distorted by coercive power relations can and ought to be resisted by those who are oppressed by them. In different circumstances that allow self-reflection and critique, "insiders" can reconstruct new traditions of practice and of understanding. Elliot (1988) elaborates on what these "different circumstances" might be in terms of teacher education research. A form of participatory research in which "the outsider [acts] as reflective teacher educator" and "the insider as reflective teacher" (p. 163) is, in Elliot's view, the most appropriate to advocacy, in that it does not exclude insiders, including pre-service teachers, from processing each other's observations or from engaging in dialogue about them. It is the "insider" who therefore acts as "broker," in exchanging information, seeking out alternative understandings of practical situations when "traditional" values and beliefs appear to fail, and thereby reconstructing traditional values and beliefs, albeit in a necessarily limited and partial way (p. 164). This model differs from "outsider as critical theorist/insider as self-reflective practitioner" (pp. 161–162), because it does not recognize the outsider as having a privileged vantage point above and beyond one's own or the insider's practical tradition.

There exists a real dilemma here for the teacher educator who fears that the self-reflection of pre-service teachers as insiders may not be "socially critical enough," or that the pre-service teacher has not had sufficient experience of teaching practice to have developed anything more than an embryonic "practical consciousness" as a teacher. Preparedness to open up a research model to discrepant data is as difficult for the researcher/outsider as it is for the researched/insider to grapple with the different viewpoints and biases of others. Yet if we are to accept Gadamer's view of the relationship between "understanding," "personality," and the social-political order, then there is no justification for the researcher-as-advocate to attempt any more intrusive role in the social practices of pre-service teachers beyond that of educational facilitator (Elliot, 1988, p. 165).

This last tale is my own account of the final reflective stages of participatory research with pre-service teachers. It is a tale that further challenges the research/teaching binary formulation of teacher educator work. The argument is not that all research must be pedagogical, but that too often teacher educators design projects with the presumption that somewhere, somehow, someone will do their pedagogical work better as a result of this or that study. Too seldom can we demonstrate how pre-service teachers actually benefited from a set of practices termed "research." In the study below, meeting/critiquing the needs of pre-service teachers is reconceptualized as a research process that is at the same time a pedagogical process, with the student needs talk (analyzed in the previous chapter) informing the negotiated curriculum in which the process occurred, not the sociopolitical agenda of the researcher.

THEORIZING TALK AS ACTION

While the language we choose to articulate our assumptions and beliefs has both a social and an active character (Austin, 1976), treatment of these two dimensions of language has tended to remain abstract (Thompson, 1984, p. 7). Thompson declares that, where analysis has occurred, there has been a tendency to emphasize form and structure at the expense of content. What is said has been overshadowed by "the semantic domain" (p. 8). Inasmuch as discourse may be understood as actual communicative practice (Miller, 1990, p. 119), it is the substance of the speech-acts of pre-service teachers and of teacher educator as facilitator that constitute the "action" of the research, rather than "doing" in the sense of field work. In embarking on this part of my teacher education research project, I understood the pre-service classroom as a social-historical site in which "speech action" occurs, a specific institutional context that enables and constrains discursive practice, and therefore as appropriate a location for this sort of inquiry as the school site.

When I began my research in the late 1980s, participatory research was generally understood to refer to one model—*action research*. Of the types of action research available to me for experimentation and modification,[1] Kemmis and McTaggart's seemed most empathic with this theoretical framework. Their definition had both a critical and a collaborative dimension that seemed crucial in achieving the goals of this study:

> Action research is a form of *collective* self-reflective inquiry undertaken by participants in social situations in order to improve the rationality and justice of their own social or educational practices and the situations in which these practices are carried out . . . the action research of the group is achieved through the *critically examined action* of individual group members. (1988, p. 5; emphasis in original)

However, since this phase of the inquiry into pre-service needs was part of a larger project informed by neo-feminist notions of research as *advocacy* or *praxis,* it was therefore, in some significant ways, different from action research, even of this critical type. This is because feminists problematize the concept of "voice" (Ellsworth, 1989; Lather, 1989), requiring us to consider who can speak for whom and how practices to discover the truth about ourselves impact on our lives (Lather, 1989, p. 28). Working "within/against" our own praxis-oriented inquiry (Lather, 1991a) is a necessary part of providing "semiotic space" for marginalized voices such as those of pre-service teachers, and for ensuring against the construction of what is in reality "a more 'with it' version of . . . intrusive surveillance" (Lather, 1989, p. 28). The challenge for feminist inquiry is "to deconstruct what IS through the process of making something else with other people" (Orner & Brennan, 1989, p. 3) whose voices are as partial and contradictory as our own (Ellsworth, 1989, p. 312). Feminists have rightly critiqued the practices of avant-garde educators for "failing to come to grips with issues of trust, risk, and the operations of fear and desire . . . around issues of identity and politics in the classroom" (Ellsworth, 1989, p. 313).

This part of my research was construed as a necessary "reciprocal" component of the much larger project of feminist praxis with pre-service teachers. What was important to me was that those pre-service teachers who served the research project by providing texts for analysis would be served by it in demonstrably beneficial ways.

Coming to grips with the urgent question raised by those who are finding voice to articulate their own fears means taking the feminist challenge of "working together across differences" (Ellsworth, 1989, p. 314) seriously enough to confront the problematic dynamics of the university classroom. Further, it means avoiding the "all too easy polemic that opposes victims to perpetrators" (Ellsworth, 1989, p. 315). In the case of pre-service teacher education, the practicum school and those who work in it can very easily be constructed as the "villain of the piece" by avant-garde teacher educators bemoaning the absence of critical pedagogy in schools, and by pre-service teachers who were under scrutiny and pressure during the field experience. "Tut-tutting" the technocrats is a most tempting game for critical academics to get undergraduates to play.

WORKING INSIDE OUT: AN INTERACTIVE RESEARCH TALE

"Playing out critique in the real" (Foucault, 1981, p. 13) involves a great deal more than wrestling with the sort of ontological or political/

relational issues mentioned above. It means confronting a host of logistical problems, not the least of which are the organizational realities of the site in which the research is located, and the "possible" in terms of what workload the participants can reasonably commit to. If the four "moments" of action research identified by Kemmis and McTaggart (1988, p. 53)—planning, acting, observing, and reflecting—were to be realized, I needed to do the sort of reconnaissance that could ensure against slippage between the research intentions and its "playing out."

Because the interactive research I conducted followed the longer process of inquiry mentioned in the previous chapter, participants had already developed a sense of being involved in a special sort of process. Therefore, thankfully, group formation (Kemmis & McTaggart, 1988, pp. 51–53) was not a problem in terms of individual identity or commitment. However, the logistics of bringing together all of the 14 pre-service participants at the same time in their university week presented an insurmountable problem. Not only did I not wish to add a further weight to their already heavy academic load, but I did not want to require significantly more of their time than other students were giving to the pre-service course. Again, the principle was that involvement in the research would be deemed a positive benefit to their professional development, not a negative and onerous commitment after the demanding practicum period, which had been their first task for the semester.

Because this phase of the research was intended to be a genuinely dialogic encounter, my own experiences of teaching successfully in secondary schools in Queensland for 19 years could not be allowed to congeal into "the truth about secondary teaching" for the participants. Given the willingness of this group of pre-service teachers, in the main, to defer to teaching "experience," as indicated in the previous tale, it would not be easy to establish "parity of esteem" for all the contributing voices. Like these authors themselves, I had to wrestle with my own constructions of self as "out in front" in order to be both an advocate and a facilitator.[2] Despite my being an opponent of an apprenticeship of immersion in pre-service training, I ran a considerable risk of immersing the group participants in my own "trade" discourse. However, my extended immersion in the analysis of the student discourse would be pedagogically useful in allowing me to privilege their texts rather than sliding into anecdotalism.

A further issue was the importance of group "ownership" of the teaching/learning situation as a series of experiences designed to spring from, and respond to, the participants' needs. If collective "action" was to be produced in the form of new knowledge about emancipatory teaching, the content of the course itself must be owned by the actors, and be generative of action. Lewis (1990) draws attention to the fact that feminist teaching practices cannot be separated from the content of the curriculum, in that "specific political moments arise exactly because of the content of the course" (p. 486). It was crucial, therefore, that the group members did not take on the role of "passive recipient" of the researcher's own "predefined" professional services, but see themselves, in Fraser's (1989) terminology, as "agents involved in interpreting their needs and shaping their life conditions" (p. 19). A negotiated curriculum was much more likely to be jointly owned and acted on than one imposed "from above." Moreover, given the sense of immediacy in the texts participants produced at the beginning of their final semester, the chances of a successful curriculum based on "what the lecturer now believes you need" were slim indeed.

The implications of this for the research meant that the writing task completed by group members at the beginning of this phase (i.e., the beginning of their final semester of the whole pre-service course), entitled "What I now believe I need," would be a major piece of reconnaissance before planning the curriculum. The concerns expressed here would be the subject matter about which we would become both more informed and more critical throughout the semester.

Working with a subset of group members, I identified three questions as the broad issues that arose from the "needs" documents:

- What field of forces constitutes the teaching environment in which we may be working next year?
- What are the possibilities for empowering action within this?
- What operational strategies will be needed to achieve this?

While these three themes would provide a framework for discussion and debate, there was no further attempt to lock in a specific agenda at this planning stage. Rather, it was agreed at the first meeting to allow an agenda to emerge from week to week, the result of concerns expressed and debates unresolved. This was to prove most responsive to group needs, as attendance and energy level indicated throughout. Far from being a laissez-faire approach, it was understood by all to be most appropriate to the present-centeredness and the state of flux that characterized participants' needs talk after their final practicum.

It was clear that "acting" and "observing" would take place to some extent simultaneously in the seminars themselves, as versions of teaching and learning were contested and rearticulated through the "speech actions" of participants. However, these phases were to come to include others who remained outside the group, as comparisons were made and pedagogical processes assessed by them and their peers elsewhere in the course. Indeed, two participants (Peter and Rita) remained in the mainstream subject "in case they missed anything," but admitted after a short time that they were attending these classes infrequently. This contrasted with their faithful attendance at the action research meetings.

Acting was not to be strictly confined to discussing/debating. Some actions were taken that involved specific sorts of data collection and distribution, and I was made aware, as the program progressed, that students outside the research project were availing themselves of information assembled and disseminated in the group. It was decided that we would all contribute to a folio of materials that were pertinent to the needs of the beginning teacher, and that this would be in constant circulation, as well as being regularly updated and augmented. All group members also kept personal notes on each session. "Minutes" of each dialogic encounter were always reconstructed onto computer file from these notes, both my own and others, within 24 hours of any session. These provided a session-by-session account of the project, showing the similarities and differences among the research participants, now reconstituted into two groups.

Another important aspect of the initial planning phase was that I disseminated to each participant a copy of all the texts, oral and written, that she or he had produced up to this point in the study. This was to allow all involved to reflect on the language they had used to talk about teacher needs. By compiling a narrative that responded to the task of elaborating "how my understanding of my needs as a teacher has changed over three years," each group member had acted to generate a new written text on which to reflect, in order to plan for the next action. My writing task as researcher/facilitator was to provide a synopsis of the purpose and structure of my thesis in accessible language (this is provided later in the chapter). Finally, I recorded participants' evaluations of this reciprocal phase in the form of taped interviews.

What became clear to me soon after this phase of "reflection-in-action" began was the fact that planning, acting, observing, and reflecting did not happen as discrete and tidy phases of research, nor did they focus on only one issue. While we were planning in terms of a suitable way forward in addressing one area of concern, other issues were at various stages of being reflected on, planned, acted on, and observed. I was beginning to experience a sense of loss of control that I had not previously felt in the study.

This might well have been interpreted as a positive sign that my role was genuinely facilitative, not engineering. Yet I was also aware of the difficulty of recording the increasing complexity of the "spiraling" of related yet disparate events that were occurring simultaneously at great speed. The spiral was more reminiscent of the widening gyre of W. B. Yeats's (1975) falcon, which "cannot hear the falconer" (p. 440), than any logical and predictable geometry. The sense of urgency these pre-service teachers brought to the task of meeting/critiquing their own needs propelled the research and the researcher along at a rate that had not been predicted, and along several paths of inquiry simultaneously. Any neat geometrical model or chronological record could not do justice to the interrelationships between "knowledges" generated or boundaries crossed. Critical and constructive analyses emerged at unpredictable times and in unforeseen ways, a reminder to the researcher that knowledge is a process of "various kinds of remakings . . . across the boundaries that ordinarily label the social, the cultural and the personal" rather than "a solid, though socially reflexive, object" (Wexler, 1987, p. 110). I could neither expect nor demand that knowledge about certain types of needs would be generated in the session devoted, in theory, to the consideration of that issue. Nor could I expect an agenda to remain "intact" from week to week—indeed, not even from hour to hour.

Further, there was a "mushrooming" effect on the tasks that I had initially set myself, as I was propelled into forums I had hitherto not anticipated engaging in. My role as discourse analyst and group facilitator was now being expanded to "beginning teacher advocate" in a range of forums, including a working party on competency-based standards and the teaching profession, teachers' union meetings about teacher unemployment, auditing new recruitment interview models being trialed by major employing authorities, and the planning of a pilot scheme in 1992 to alter the practicum experience, with supervising teachers working in the area of language and literacy.

Obviously, a week-by-week account would not be appropriate to the task of elaborating this range of experiences in terms of knowledge production. No researcher can hope to legislate what knowledge will be produced when, nor indeed should one expect a linear or even a spiraling progression to be the outcome of genuinely dialogic encounter. Often the most rewarding insights in one area came in the context of debating a quite different issue on the agenda. The decision was made, therefore, to present an analysis of the way knowledge was generated in response to the three core questions above by examining sites of struggle that emerged as pivotal in the needs talk now being articulated in the groups. These were identified as five—the practicum experience, the recruitment process, critiquing the literature, rereading personal texts, and activating our negotiated curriculum. No attempt was made, in the elaborations below, to give any chronological framework to our struggle with these dilemmas. Rather, the "order" of their elaboration is informed by the degree of urgency of the needs talk the group was perceived to use in response to them.

THE PRACTICUM EXPERIENCE

It was evident in these first sessions that the power relations of the practicum were of overwhelming and universal concern. The discussions seemed, in general terms, to bear out the truth of Beauchamp and Parsons' (1989) assertion that "the situation [in the practicum] is schizophrenic" (p. 164), with the student teacher both fully in charge and yet never in charge, because she or he "can never make the crucial decisions" (p. 164). An emotionally charged discussion of the power relations of the just-completed field experience gave way to a more cogent analysis of the types of relationships experienced.

The first categories of power relations generated out of the discussion was that of "coexistence" (autonomy without acknowledgment). Trevor and Rosemarie both claimed to have experienced this. They felt unhindered but also relatively unmotivated, receiving little acknowledgment of, or thanks for, the job done. This seemed to be particularly important to Trevor, who felt he had worked hard for an unimpressive mark and no thanks. Further, he felt, as did others, that he was given good reason to suppose that his mark would be high, but that the recorded result was just mediocre.

Others felt that they had been involved in "empowering partnerships" and had a genuine sense of working successfully alongside another successful professional. Mandy, Melanie, and Vera all expressed delight with their sense of being involved as fellow teachers. While they were sympathetic with others, expressing the view that they had "the luck of the draw" in terms of supervising teachers, they returned with high energy for full-time teaching. Vera noted the importance of the ethos of prac school. She felt that she worked in a democratic and open environment that was not characteristic of most secondary schools.

In contrast, a third "category" was generated much later than the first session devoted to discussion of the practicum. This "untidy" emergent data is characteristic of the action research process as I have experienced it, despite my best attempts to ensure that the process of inquiry was systematic and logical, in accordance with the dictates of making inquiry public. One student, Andrea, spoke of "a partnership of powerlessness" in that she was "accepted as one of the victims" in her prac school. After she had experienced a rather traumatic encounter with an abusive student, "The staff was lovely to me and even brought me flowers. I felt like I was one of them." Andrea agreed with the proposition put forth by Roxanne, myself, and others that this camaraderie was built on her joining their ranks as "another victim," a fellow traveler as disenfranchised as themselves. This was how "real" teaching might be constructed by a "defeated" professional group. She had not been supported at the time of the crisis by the supervising teacher in the room, whose response was to tell her not to respond with "What did you say?" to such abuse, but then offered nothing further than "You can't do anything with that kid."

A most frustrating "category" seemed to be that of "apprenticeship" (a sense of working "under"). Dee was obviously very upset by her experience with some staff. While she appreciated the time taken by one staff member to guide her, she felt that her own skills and her desires to practice inquiry-based learning were frustrated. She alluded to the possibility of jealousy in one case—that she achieved better student response than the teacher did. She expressed a decision not to become a teacher. This surprised me, given the degree of Dee's enthusiasm throughout the course and the frequency of her visits to my office for a chat. Marilyn also experienced a sense of "working under," but not with such a manifest negativity.

Finally, mention was made of the need for a category called "opposition" (a sense of working against). While Ken said very little about his prac experiences, he seized on this category very quickly and with definite nonverbals when it was suggested. He expressed the view that there was a fundamental disagreement between him and his supervising teachers. This was not elaborated on at the time, though in the final interview Ken said:

> I found it easy being a student . . . what's been difficult for me is doing the prac. . . . I went to the wrong school. . . . I sort of wanted to go back to the textbook . . . we didn't get on. . . . I think this is where the whole course falls down . . . there needs to be more said about prac. Their attitude was, "We'll step back and you take over" . . . teach their lessons their way with no help from them . . . the fact is I think they're going to

ask me to do third year prac again, so I won't have the option
of teaching anyway.

While others in the group expressed frustration with the role of student to which they returned after the practicum, Ken indicated his
preference for the student role, after the traumatic experience of having
failure recorded in his prac report.

I commented on what I had perceived, during my time as a
teacher educator, to be "Final-year Fatigue" in terms of the energy
many final-year students, including members of this group, seemed to
lack after a strong enthusiasm in the first and second years. Melanie
expressed the belief that final-year students experience a particular
form of pressure that is the result of having to cope with a paradox.
They are considered to be at the height of their "undergraduate teaching powers" by this stage and are therefore "assessed harder," yet are
"only student teachers" in terms of status. She regards this as an explanation for the apparent third- (final-) year malaise. This example of
"schizophrenia" is consistent with the findings of Beauchamp and Parsons (1989, p. 164). Yet this was not the experience of all. Those who
had claimed to work in empowering partnerships at prac school felt
more energetic, at least for their future teaching, if not for continued
university study.

The issue of the practicum was to generate an opportunity to be
involved with teachers for whom the practicum had also become a
political issue. Two group members, Roxanne and Vera, made me
aware of, and engineered for me an invitation to, a meeting with 14
English teachers, including a number of department coordinators, in
which the power relations of the prac emerged as a central agenda
item. Here, the issue of the powerlessness of the pre-service teacher
was dealt with somewhat defensively on the part of the practicing
teachers. Not only did they stress the importance of pre-service teachers' taking their own initiatives to change the situation, but they indicated that worse "surveillance" was to follow in their first and second
year of service.

I was pleased at this meeting to see Roxanne and Vera counter so
well the propositions that the power relations of the practicum were
essentially of the pre-service teacher's making, and that success was a
matter of "being a more assertive personality," rather than any issue to
do with the power relations within structures of schools and school
knowledge. I also noted what I took to be a defensive response to my
indicating a desire to become more involved in a teaching partnership,
not simply an inspectorial presence at the back of the prac room. How-

ever, this was not universal, and it was clear that some of the secondary teachers present were open to a more genuine pedagogical partnership with teacher educators than currently existed. An outcome of this meeting was the creation of a student teacher support group, of which I was a founding member, to design a pilot "partnership" model to be tried out in English curriculum at a selected group of local secondary schools. This totally unforeseen development was in some ways an indirect product of a process in which a teacher educator and her charges understood themselves to be embarked on a mutual task. Not only was I able to act as an advocate for pre-service teachers and support them in their challenges to their future colleagues, but they likewise were able to act as advocates for teacher educators who attempt to engage in more partnership-oriented practicum experiences in the future.

Having "acted" in the prac situation, having observed its consequences for themselves and reflected on the possibilities that might be in it for experiencing the practicum differently, these pre-service teachers were now involved with me at the level of "the real" in a particular group of schools. Our speech actions had led us to planning for, and engagement with, secondary teachers who would become part of the planning, acting, observing, and reflecting process in the design of a more empowering field experience for future pre-service teachers.

THE RECRUITMENT PROCESS

The issue of what might constitute empowering knowledge for beginning teachers was clearly central, not only as a result of the deconstruction of the practicum, but also within a context in which they would be competing with thousands of experienced teachers, currently unemployed, for a career with the state's department of education. The fact that the recruitment interview by the staffing officers of the department of education was imminent directed attention to the many negative myths and anecdotes that had caused consternation to pre-service teachers in the past. This group was no less immune to fears that their services would be undervalued by the "bureaucrats" who would make the decision as to whether they would be "hired." The connotation of a "public servant" was a negative one in this context. It was clear in both groups that the participants' attention was being directed toward life after the practicum in which they expected to find themselves powerless or defenseless.

The immediacy and importance of a successful recruitment interview could not be ignored. The fact that these interviews were held over a timespan of several weeks during this praxis phase provided a very strong argument for keeping the agenda flexible from week to week. However, it could not be allowed to marginalize other important issues in the curriculum we were negotiating, and also had to be subject to our own critique. It would be tempting to change the agenda into simply trying to predict and provide "what the department wants." Again possibilities could be lost through attempting to "second-guess" and imitate the "ideal teacher" as defined by the department of education, regardless of personal pedagogical commitment. While desirable elements of "performance" in a challenging professional situation such as this must not be ignored, it was also important to observe and reflect on the very speech acts that were constructing pre-service teachers as once again the "victims" of processes controlled by others. Lather's (1991a) notion of working "within/against" was again applicable here.

A pilot scheme for recruitment to the department of education presented opportunities for me as a teacher educator to act as an advocate on the pre-service teachers' behalf, and to contribute positively to critiquing as well as demythologizing the interview process. The new format being piloted was, in essence, a "revamping" of the type of interviews to be conducted to select potential teaching recruits. My role as a teacher educator enabled me to seek out the opportunity to "audit" an interview and pass on any feedback to the group. I was disappointed to find that my own teacher education institution had not taken the opportunity of auditing simulated interviews, so I availed myself of an opportunity elsewhere.

The interview, and the power relations in which it is located, were then to be an important object of analysis for the group over the duration of this action research phase, in that the recruitment interview was experienced by everyone in the groups during this time, and was a unique and differentiating experience for all. Just as the power relations of the practicum were to be an on-going issue for deconstruction, so too the power relations of the recruitment process and the assumptions that appeared to inform it would furnish a rich source of issues for critique and construct. It was pleasing to note that few if any group members gave the impression of being intimidated or overwhelmed by the experience, a result, they agreed, of the sort of critique that had occurred in the respective groups and the information I was able to glean about the questions likely to be asked. Again, it was critique and construct in combination that was most effective in the pedagogical process.

CRITIQUING THE LITERATURE

While the practicum and the interview were two important situations on which the group focused as "real-life" experiences, decisions were also made to read and critique a range of materials that might be useful in exploring pedagogies of possibility for the beginning teacher. It was decided by the group that there were three types of texts that ought to be subjected to critical scrutiny. These were research that purported to elaborate how "beginning teaching" was experienced, documents pertaining to current trends and changes in secondary education and in teachers' professional work, and the participants' own developing "stories" about teaching.

In the case of beginning-teacher research literature, a bibliography of readings had been provided in the "mainstream" subject outline. We decided to review these and to add a few that were not included but looked promising. Each group member took responsibility for critiquing one or more articles pertinent to research into beginning teaching, and sharing her or his critique with the group. The task was to identify how this article might inform the needs of a beginning teacher.

"Audience" was to emerge as a central issue here, with the group members distinguishing quite perceptively those articles written for them. They were quick to denounce articles that appeared to be written for academics rather than for them. For example, Zeichner and Tabachnick's (1981) "Are the Effects of University Education Washed Out by School Experience?" was critiqued by Melanie as inaccessible to students and clearly written for an academic audience, as was Slee's (1988) "Policy Development: Discipline or Control?" Other articles were dismissed as pretty much "common sense" and even "simplistic," e.g., Boynton, Di Geronimo, and Gustafson's (1985) "A Basic Survival Guide for New Teachers," as critiqued by Margaret. What became apparent was that neither avant-garde discourse of the type used by Zeichner and Tabachnick nor simplistic formulae of the sort that characterized Boynton and associates were acceptable to the groups. The academic language of my own texts would doubtless fit into the "inaccessible" category. This was one of the reasons I had for writing a student "version" of the research tale about their needs.

An article that did generate quite a deal of discussion was Bullough's (1987) "Planning and the First Year of Teaching." The four stages Bullough identifies in professional development—fantasy, survival, mastery, and impact—were considered, particularly with regard to whether they were true of all beginning teachers, and whether the sequence begins before the first year of teaching service. Notes made by Roxanne about her own concerns paralleled particular items in the article such as "because you fear chaos you are reluctant to relax" (p. 56). For Roxanne, too, it was "the fear of chaos more than the reality of the disruptive classroom" that was most troubling. "Identifying and routinizing activities and instructional stages appropriate for the students and personally satisfying" was identified by her and by others as "something I'd like to know."

This seems to me to be the point at which teacher education programs desert potentially socially critical teachers like Roxanne. They do not take up in any substantive way the issue of how pre-service teachers might identify and establish activities for their daily teaching in mainstream schools. In order to use pedagogies as forms of resistance within such settings, certain procedures and practices would be needed to ensure that a new teacher's own pedagogical processes can be competently carried out.

Ken's response to a collection of interviews with beginning teachers (Warner & Swindell, n.d.) was that it pleased him to note that his concerns were being shared by so many others. This might be reinforcement of the notion of a "partnership of powerlessness" alluded to in earlier discussion of the practicum. While this could give temporary respite from feeling unique in terms of an inability to solve problems, it did not augur well for acting as a change agent in terms of the power relations of schools.

A prominent theme in the discussion of pre-service problems in teacher education literature is that of "transition shock" (Corcoran, 1981). The matter of whether the shock need be violent or traumatic, or, indeed, was a necessary part of first-year teaching at all was discussed. Trevor felt that Corcoran's article did not help in examining the extent of this phenomenon, since it was a case study of someone he believed to be naive in the extreme. Again, the participants did not construct the writer as empathic with the first-year teacher as actor, but took the research to be a continuation of the surveillance to which they themselves had been subjected during the practicum. As Trevor pointed out, there was no indication in the article as to how the research was of benefit to the "researched" beginning teacher in this case. The criticisms Tripp (1990) levels at researchers for the predominance of research "that aims to produce knowledge principally for academics to use" (p. 63) appeared to be strongly affirmed in discussion of this article.

"The Teacher's Communicative Competence: The First Day of School" (Brooks, 1985) proved to be very useful, not so much for its content as for its not-so-hidden curriculum. This article contrasted a novice with an experienced teacher in terms of activity selection and sequence in a first lesson. While John was pleased by the focus on the first lesson, he was not so pleased by the models (both experienced and inexperienced) that were elaborated, since his subject discipline of Drama did not seem represented. He felt that the more experienced teacher seemed to provide the dullest classroom experiences for the students, in a technocratic model of "efficiency" intended to contrast positively with the inefficiency of the novice. Both teaching models were rejected as inappropriate to first-day work. The issue of "first day first class" was raised as a result of John's critique and the theme of the article. Both groups responded enthusiastically to the suggestion that this matter be pursued in a later session.

What was most useful about this process of critique was not so much the information pre-service teachers gained from the readings as the ways in which they made the research "findings" problematic. The issue of voice, of who was speaking for whom and with what pay-off for whom, emerged as crucial. The groups seemed to engage in the reading tasks much more diligently when they did not have to approach the readings as *the canon* of teacher education, but as partial tales whose legitimacy they could decide for themselves.

REREADING PERSONAL TEXTS

Another important source of knowledge about power relations came from the texts produced by all the participants as researcher and researched. As discourse analyst, I had the important task of reading each participant's own story constructed out of her or his oral and written texts, and producing my own "story" about their collective experience of pre-service preparation. I understood my own narrative as partial and open to the critique of the other participants in the group as my co-theorists, as it would not be if written in academic jargon and remaining within the domain of "thesis-writing." My narrative (as follows) was disseminated to the group for critique:

MY STORY ABOUT GROUP "NEEDS TALK"

My analysis of your stories about your needs is informed by my own belief that teaching is a political and moral as well as a technical endeavor, and that powerful teachers have powerful students. It is also made in the context of themes in pre-service educational research and development, in particular:

- Pre-service teachers enter university humanistic/idealistic/soft and leave realistic/custodial/hardened/cynical, or leave university idealistic and become "realistic" in their first year of service.
- Pre-service teachers see teacher knowledge in terms of "theory," which they associate with university and irrelevance, or "technique/content," which they associate with prac school and relevance.
- Pre-service teachers are "survival-focused," not student-focused.

Reading the narratives of the group has led me to understand power relations as a crucial issue in pre-service preparation. I believe that the above research themes and the stories told by the group both appear to suggest that there is a time in the socialization of a pre-service teacher when she becomes aware of her own powerlessness. At the time this occurs, she experiences a sapping of confidence and an increasing cynicism about the value of what she is doing, unless at the same time she is able to understand the power relations which have shaped her understanding of what she does and her role as a teacher. All educators believe at times that either they themselves or "the system" is at fault when they feel constrained by the sorts of knowledge that has or has not been available to them and the sort of relationships they have entered into in educational contexts.

Let me offer my version of teacher socialization, informed by this theory, for your constructive critique:

Anticipatory Socialization (Pre-university)

Pre-service teachers enter first year after being "on the receiving end" (Mandy) of the educational process. They bring with them a vision of teachers as powerful inasmuch as they have appeared to exercise power, positive or negative or both, over their own lives. They remember significant experiences, good and bad, that they had with their own teachers, and these inform what they do or do not want to become. These can remain quite strong. (A question for you: Are they weaker if a pre-service teacher is older upon entry?) What is most important at this stage is a sense of the power of teachers that derives from the residual "student" point of view. Associated with this is often a romantic ideal of what they wanted of their own past teachers, especially in terms of understanding.

Early Times (Before Prac)

In the first three semesters of the three-year course, pre-service teachers often learn about the complexity of the teaching act through "dollops" of theory and/or integrated "foundational" studies and introduction to curriculum. They are likely to come to believe that teachers are not as powerful as they had thought, and may even be depressed by the amount that needs to be learned to be a good teacher. They may begin to see the difficulties of meeting all the demands that learning makes. Some are more disturbed by this than others. They may even begin to develop an "oppositional" voice to authoritarian teacher culture (Roxanne). This is reflected on as undermining confidence in teaching in mainstream schooling but is later understood as "better in second year than first year out" (Roxanne). Many begin to be impatient to get into "the real world" of teaching, and begin to see the demands of on-campus university studies as a distraction to their training as teachers. All still experience the power of teachers, in the form of either teacher educators who can keep them jumping through academic hoops, some of which seem inexplicably unrelated to the act of teaching, or their memories of past teachers. They tend to prefer and defer to those lecturers who seem to have had some actual experience in schools and who seem competent. While lecturers are powerful in that they credential students, failure is known to be fairly unlikely once they are "in the pipeline." Pre-service teachers come to believe that the big challenges will not be at university, and that "academic success" will not translate into "teaching power." Many continue to be delighted by the self-knowledge they have generated in this time—"I came as one of the white middle-class masses" (Vera)—and critical thinking skills they have developed (Rita, Mandy). They may begin to understand university culture, particularly in terms of its critique of schooling practices, as antithetical to school culture. Yet the "acid" test of actual teaching is known to reside in the classroom.

The First Intensive Prac

While lecturers have "inspectorial" powers over pre-service teachers on prac, supervisory teachers are now understood as ultimately more powerful in terms of the requirements they may have and the models they may provide for teaching and learning. Some group members seemed acutely attuned to the advice of their supervisors, particularly the criticisms—"Successes are gone. The problems are still there to be handled the next day." (Margaret)—viewing their own inexperience as a huge handicap and deferring to their supervisor's classroom experience as a superior form of power/knowledge (Ken). This may, on return to university studies, be manifest in an increased and expressed cynicism about university demands in general, especially if lecturers made apparently arbitrary judgments based on fleeting and "faceless" prac visits (Trevor). For those who felt acutely aware of deficits in their content knowledge while on prac, university courses are critiqued as failing to offer "content relevant to the in-school situation" (Peter). Others return buoyed up and jubilant about their introductory teaching experiences (Marilyn), and experience a strong commitment as a result of their sense of having power to affect the lives of their students. Perceptive critiques of the power relations of the practicum are rare (Roxanne is the exception), as there appears to be a tendency to presume that powerlessness experienced on prac was unpleasant yet somehow appropriate to the lack of status implied by the designation "student teacher." Where classroom power was understood by the prac supervisor as equating with custodialism, and where creativity was discouraged, concern for managerial techniques increased or was critiqued. Understandings of the communication process are thereafter more likely to be expressed as working "in front" to "pass over content" or "get information across," or "get them to . . .," and the two-way language that accompanied the romantic ideal of power-sharing with a teacher diminishes.

Post-prac University Studies ("Back to School")

Between the second- and third-year practicum, there is change in the tenor of student critiques. It is not that idealism disappears, but that the belief that the rest of the course will solve all the remaining problems for them as teachers is seriously under threat. There is a sense that university is only providing "more of the same," and that heavier assessment is the only qualitative distinction that can now be made about the nature of the third-year offering as distinct from the first or second year. It is almost as though the university has attempted to reassert its power through more assessment—not begin to relinquish it through more meaningful postpracticum learnings. Regardless of whether the political nature of the teaching act has been perceived or articulated up to this point, between second year and third year there seems to be a growing resentment of the "quantity-equals-quality" logic that appears to accompany requirements for third-year studies.

Third-Year Prac and Beyond

The third-year prac is perceived to be the ultimate "acid test" in that it brings with it a set of expectations that are paradoxical. As expressed by Melanie, it is a time when undergraduates are regarded as at the height of their pre-service teaching powers yet at the same time are "only student teachers." Assessment is tougher now, yet status does not grow concomitantly with this. A number of pre-service teachers experienced for the first time the timidity of supervising teachers in making decisions, and their preference for awarding mediocre grades despite oral approval and even high praise (Trevor). This may be the wheel turning full circle in that many who have acquiesced in their own powerlessness are now making the decision to disempower others, not through "hard" grading but through their very insecurity about committing to an evaluation of a pre-service teacher's performance. It is in the contradiction between what is said and what is written as a permanent record that the powerlessness of the profession is revealed.

This prac period is a real watershed for future teachers. Some have more than two years enthusiasm dashed by their experience of staffroom and professional culture (Dee). Others have confirmed for themselves all they ever felt about this as a vocation (Melanie, Rita, Mandy, Vera). Some come back to university with a sense of having their labor exploited, or at least unacknowledged (Trevor, Peter). Where they experienced a sense of genuine partnership with teaching staff, rather than co-existing with them or working under or against them, hopes remain high for future success.

My Concern as a Teacher Educator

While I must now acknowledge all the problems in the conceptualizing of pre-service courses, my overwhelming concern is now helping my students to understand the power relations in which teachers work without being defeated by them. I am concerned that those who do not experience teaching as political (i.e., having to do with power relations) may suffer the "reality shock" that is understood to be experienced by first-year teachers. This often makes them abandon declared ideals and innovative possibilities in favor of "grim realism" and pupil-control ideology. These beginning teachers often have a strong moral commitment to helping others, but may be distracted from planning rigorous and meaningful sequences of learnings by a form of romantic individualism that ignores power relations and their effects. They may, as a consequence, end up the victim, despite their genuine desire to save student "victims." They may also blame themselves for failure, or crusade for change in ways that are well-intentioned yet naive. This will often be quickly pointed out by "experienced" staff members. They may feel that the answer is to work harder when they are already doing too much, and "burn out" very quickly. Or they may blame university courses in retrospect for giving them an impossible vision of teaching excellence.

On the other hand, I am concerned that some pre-service teachers never see or are challenged to experience for themselves the process of empowering teaching because they understand themselves as simply "handing over knowledge" as though it were a package or a relay baton. Certain subject disciplines appear to frame knowledge only as content and never as process. What students learn in this framework is more likely to be that learning is basically a boring but necessary thing to do for credentialing purposes. Living is something else ("The geranium on the window sill just died but the teacher kept right on teaching"). The role of a teacher becomes managerial, not facilitative. Students become faceless receptacles for "pouring in the right stuff." Teachers thereby create their own prisons and believe their own myths (e.g., "You can't do anything creative with this class!"). These myths are self-fulfilling prophecies and tedious, chalk-and-talk lessons are how they are often manifest in classrooms. Often these teachers presume (wrongly, in my view) that what they are doing is something "neutral" or objective, unlike the "biased" information of other teachers. They can contribute to the destruction of learning pleasure despite being very nice people themselves. They are quick to seize on the "quiet is good" agenda and are often well prepared with anchoring work that "keeps heads down." It is not that quiet or "heads down" is wrong, just that it is only a very limited part of the learning process. The result is an imitative ethos in schools and a generation of people who are incapable of higher order thinking for themselves.

In conclusion, pre-service teachers can experience powerlessness in first year, on the first prac, as the pre-service course progresses, or as beginning teachers. The chances of never feeling powerless are slim, given what counts as legitimate schooling. What I would hope for is that pre-service teachers can acknowledge the power relations in which they, as educators, now work and will work, and that they not wish them away, ignore them, or be defeated by them. Any of these options can only mean powerlessness for undergraduates as future professionals and for the future students they teach. However, pre-service teachers can work toward a form of power/knowledge that gives them energy and power instead of taking it away. The task is to analyze what this might be, and access it—fast.

THE GROUP'S REACTION

The response of the participants, particularly those in the Wednesday group, was, in the main, acquiescence. They accepted my account as "the truth about pre-service socialization" and were reticent to criticize it. I realized the truth of Ellsworth's (1989) claim that "the essentially paternalistic project of traditional education" had denied students any opportunity of exercising an authentic oppositional voice (p. 307), and that, as a result, they would be unlikely to overturn the practices of years in the space of a week, despite the fact that it was their own texts on which my "partial" narrative was based. What was interesting, however, was the fact that they focused quickly on the only question posed in the story: Are they (childhood memories of teachers) weaker if a pre-service teacher is older on entry? The mature-aged students in both groups (Roxanne, Ken, Margaret) responded, "I wanted to answer that!" and proceeded to do so, arguing that the "uniqueness" of the experience of schooling causes it to remain sharp in the mind regardless of age. I decided that, in the future, I would present further contributions of my own in an interrogative rather than in expository text. In this way, I might be able to address the power relations in my own classroom that were limiting the genuine dialogic possibilities of the pedagogy.

My second attempt to engage the group members as cotheorists was, therefore, to pose questions about the constructions of teaching that appeared to emerge and to change in the texts they had been producing over the three years. This time the groups were much livelier, and of more assistance in helping me understand the meanings they gave to their experiences than during our first attempt at cotheorizing. As I presented to the group my analysis of their metaphorical constructions of teaching over time, I asked them to respond to my questions of clarification. For example, Peter responded to my clarification of a rationale for the teacher-as-actor metaphor by focusing on how "micro-teaching" constructs teacher work. Peter saw microlessons as more influential in the construction of teaching as performance than prac. He argued that this was where they had been encouraged to conceive of their own role as acting out a part in front of an audience. An early prac of observation served to reinforce this notion.

The metaphor of a nest-building phase caused much comment in the second group, both lighthearted and otherwise. They agreed that they were now "grabbing" for bits and pieces, swapping with others and "on the lookout" for materials and resources. This was universal, regardless of political stance. Later, Rita spoke of a further phase at the end of the entire course, a "garage sale" of ideas, assumptions, and beliefs in which professional knowledge is prioritized, structured, and often discarded in the transition from "student teacher" to "teacher." She saw herself making conscious decisions to "jettison excess baggage." This did not seem to be motivated by a technicist view of teaching in Rita's case, given the tenor of comments in her final interview.

Members of the group agreed that the earliest texts tended to construct the desirable teacher as "mutual friend." The important issue, however, was whether this was now perceived as inappropriately naive or whether it was in fact closer to student needs than later constructions of "teacher." It was clear that some participants had deserted this earlier image while others had asserted it more vociferously in their texts over time. The seeds of critical debate were already written in the texts. My task as facilitator was simply to pose the question of the appropriateness of some "versions" over others.

The metaphor of "up in front" was identified as crucial in its depiction of the separation of teacher from student. Group members experimented with new metaphors such as teaching "down behind" and tried to picture themselves adopting a different physical position in relation to students. Would it be possible to teach successfully from "down behind"? Could "pushing students up" be an appropriate metaphor for facilitating student learning? The power of their own school experiences and of the practicum in reinforcing the up-in-front image were recognized by participants here, as was the extent to which hierarchical teacher models have been absorbed by all of us as commonsense articulations of teacher work. They also acknowledged that the process in which they were currently engaged was much more acceptable and relevant to their own needs than a lecture format. What had to be confronted was a seeming paradox: that up-in-front was held to be most inappropriate for their own learning yet most appropriate for the learning of their future students.

Throughout the duration of this process I tried to resist force-feeding on social justice or intellectual bullying. Rather than the power of the lecturer's logic or personality or desire to persuade, it is the process itself that generates new pedagogical knowledge, because it is through this process that "second-order action research" is achieved, with teacher "insiders" now becoming outsider-facilitators of the teacher educators' professional learning (Elliot, 1988, p. 165). For me, in particular, it demonstrated that the power of the process of negotiated self-reflection was greater than any selection of "experience" anecdotes I might have believed to be a relevant curriculum. This is not to argue that my own teaching experience is unimportant in the process. I merely wish to point out that it is a resource, not to be imposed "from above" as the model for others to imitate.

ACTIVATING OUR NEGOTIATED CURRICULUM

This "reflection-in-action" research phase is open to negotiation. This could be argued to be potentially its greatest strength or greatest weakness. Certainly, as facilitator I found it to be the most challenging aspect of the whole process of inquiry. A considerable risk existed of a critical agenda being "hijacked" for purposes other than social reconstruction. As facilitator, I had to ensure that potentially depoliticizing or romantic articulations of the teaching/learning experience did not go unchallenged.

An example of this emerges in the request on the part of many members of both groups to spend some time on "assertiveness" skills. Instead of moving away from a critical agenda to a list of do's and don'ts, the issue of assertiveness was taken up in terms of the question "What is it that we are trying to assert?" This provided a link with the participants' own textual constructions of "teacher." If I understand teacher as "actor," then I am trying to assert that I am a good actor. If teacher means "industrial worker," then I should be asserting myself as a hard/productive worker, or as putting out "a better product," and so on. The notion that "assertiveness" can be donned like a suit of new clothes was critiqued by means of a discussion of those assumptions and beliefs that "assert" themselves in our teaching practice. Again, this demonstrated the extent to which the various elements of course construction were engaging as *con*texts in theorizing our own pedagogical work.

If it was possible to predict anything about the negotiated curriculum that would emerge, it would be that the issue of classroom "disruption" was bound to find its way onto the agenda. Indeed, it was the group member who identified himself as disruptive who was, some would argue also predictably, the most enthusiastic about this agenda item. Again, however, John's very self-designation as disruptive would be a useful means of initiating a discussion of therapeutic and managerial constructions of "upset"[3] students and the way these depoliticize the problem or blame the victim. This was not intended to play down the very real and negative effects of behavioral disruption of classrooms, but to contextualize discussion in order that it did not degenerate into seeking out recipes for "faceless teaching" that denied issues of race, poverty, and gender.

In inquiring into John's own biography as disruptive and into the reasons for this, a more empathic view of the frustrations of those marginalized by school culture became possible. In this way, the labeling of "upset" students that derives from either social pathology or human engineering models of education could be challenged. The ways that reconceptualizing students as clients might create a different ethos in the classroom, one less likely to lead to alienation and resistance of the disruptive kind, were then analyzed. Understanding the relationship between motivation and disruption was crucial in working toward a more active but less disrupted classroom atmosphere. In conflating noise with disruption and silence with work, popular discourse about teaching and learning was perceived to contribute to, rather than militate against, a state of alienation as the norm in classrooms. The group members were themselves engaging in *active* learning, which was noisy yet not negative, rowdy yet not resistant, divergent yet not discordant. Just as I, as researcher/facilitator, had feared the very loss of control that would establish the credibility of this stage of inquiry as a pedagogical process, so too did these teachers have to wrestle with the issue of handing over pedagogical power to others.

The "others" alluded to here is a category inclusive of the parents of future students. Relations with parents was a source of concern for this relatively young group of people. Not only did they identify the problem of being a 20-year-old "authority figure" attempting to relate to 40-year-olds, but the issue of insecurity in terms of their own knowledge base and knowledge of their students worried them. Again it was the group's ability to tap into the experiences of their own families that was of assistance here. Rosemarie, as a young woman from a rural town, described her mother's very active role in the school there, indicating that such a level of involvement was typical of small rural communities. As a parent herself, Margaret had educational concerns that were also brought forward for analysis. Mythologies that exist for teachers regarding parents and for parents regarding teachers were thereby addressed and "unpacked" in order to develop a more enabling approach to parent-teacher relations.

The three issues elaborated briefly above are by no means an exhaustive list of topics the group participants sought to explore. Other issues, including new assessment procedures, and industrial, legal, and pedagogical matters, were explored through the development of the folio and its circulation as well as through discussion. Issues were revisited as a result of group observation and further reflection. A typical remark from group members at the beginning of a session was "I was thinking about what we were talking about last week and. . . . "

Dee alludes to the importance of this reflective process in her final interview:

> In [the alternative subject] they're not finding out what they're really capable of . . . they're not sort of sitting down and trying to evaluate themselves. . . . I think this one, like what we've been doing with you, you get out of your class, I'm talking here on Friday mornings, and you sit and wonder, shit, yeah, am I really like that? Do I really want to be on that sort of wave length? Do I want to sort of teach that way?

Given that this phase of my research was motivated by the notion that the participants would understand themselves to have been beneficiaries of the research process, I want to evaluate the process using the comments of the participants themselves.

It became evident in the final interviews that the distinction between "telling" and "being told" had become a very important issue for these pre-service teachers. Having been in a situation of telling during the practicum, or at least acting in the capacity of professionals for six weeks, they very much resented the "as-you-were" rationale of university offerings that follows on the heels of this long prac period. While "in-servicing" was now more appropriate to the change of role they had undergone, with the exception of this research experience, they found no qualitative change in the pedagogical process that awaited them on their return to the pre-service offerings of the university campus. The following remarks were telling evidence of this:

> It's good coming back to someone like yourself and writing down what you feel is, um like not wrong, aw, well it is, it is a wrong. I think we've been gypped. So it's good coming back and telling someone because in the University they don't have that . . . you can go up to someone like in the Admin and tell them about it but I'm pretty sure they just click it away like that [clicks fingers]. You're just one voice in the crowd and that's all you'll ever be. I think it is important that we should come back and tell someone with some ground behind them. . . . I would like to see a different approach in the lecturers here. When you sit through the lecture, you ask yourself why did I bother? (John)

> It's very hard to come back from final third-year prac and put yourself into a student situation again because you've just

done a six-week bloc and you've been up there presenting and doing classes and teaching and you're in that sort of teacher mode, and then to get back and then you've got, right, deadlines, "I want you to see me about this." It's like, who am I? I always expected our final semester to be something really special and things would be much more equal and equitable but you've still got that big power thing between lecturer and student. Instead of being peers, that helps you to get out and do things well. Like we've been saying in lectures, I've been too busy thinking, "Oh God, what do I need and what should I look for?" (Andrea)

I mean you go back to every lecturer and the lecturer goes, "Oh, how was prac?" and you tell them for the first five minutes and then it's straight into course work and all the, um, that background knowledge that you've gained and experience can be used to further your skills and to pick up holes where you've found in prac and all that could be used in the last semester. . . . Now we've got the experience yet you don't hear anything about it. (Peter)

Everyone's saying, like people that are doing TS [Teaching Studies] the other way, are saying like they're just not getting what they want out of it. I mean what they thought it was going to be and what it is are completely different things. We've got an idea of what we want and by the time we've got to third year there are things that haven't been dealt with and no one asks us what we want to do about it. . . . If it's interesting enough and useful enough, everyone's gonna come. (Melanie)

Roxanne, too, identified something of a "broken-record" effect in terms of the pedagogy and type of tasks still required by lecturers that did not seem geared to her own professional growth:

The other extreme to ours is courses like a lecturer that I have, where it's still a two-hour lecture. That subject is, even though it doesn't have to be, is just a theory subject. It's caused a lot of trouble. . . . I'm not fighting it . . . my mind's graduated. My mind's off, it's gone . . . when they hand you another gender and society paper you say, yeah yeah yeah, I know [laughs]. Well, I think part of it is that you can take up the issues that you want to do. By now, I think, by third year we've all sort of developed our priorities . . . there's a lot of the political . . . if you're being lectured to and you're being told, "Here are the four assignment topics," it's really limiting. . . . I can pick things out of texts and put them into an essay no problem, that's easy. But I want something that challenges me. I think we should be in a position now of creating knowledge. (Roxanne)

Again, the schizophrenia alluded to by Beauchamp and Parsons (1989, p. 164) was manifest in the very strong sense these young people now had of competing "realities":

It really is two different worlds. Coming back, you're taking your notes down alright and you must learn this poet for your exam . . . you feel like you're being babied, it really devalues you . . . you're sort of thinking, "Oh, oh what am I doing here?" It's really sort of taking away your . . . ah, anything that you have to say, anything that might be worthwhile. It's like, you don't have anything to say, you're a student now, I'm the lecturer so just listen and take notes fast, you know. It's a real chop-change. (Mandy)

Nevertheless, Mandy went on to make it clear that she was not seeking total autonomy in her struggle "out of the dark":

With our Drama subjects, I feel it's probably the opposite, where they just left us completely um "Go and do this, we don't want to know you," they really have, and that's been, sort of, that's the opposite. It's still nice to have that bit of guidance. . . . We still need some sort of guiding light. (Mandy)

Rita and Peter, who chose to remain in the mainstream subject, made clear their preference for the pedagogical processes employed in the action research process over those used in their mainstream curriculum:

I don't think other groups have taken into account that we do have some experience and some knowledge, I'm not saying a lot, but we have had experiences in prac that we could bring into lectures. If you want to bring up a situation, you're always beaten back, it's like, "We don't want to hear about it," you know, "we're teaching you about teaching so don't butt in and tell us what you already know." It's been very much that, oh you know, "I am a lecturer and therefore I have more knowledge than you," whereas I find in this group we all bring in different situations and things we have experienced and they're seen as valid and they're seen as things that we can all learn from and that's what I've enjoyed is listening to other people's tales of prac and other experiences and thinking, well, that could be me and would I handle it that way or would I do something different. (Rita)

In [the alternative subject] we talked about what was in the Beginning Teacher Book and the students did their seminars and we all sat there really bored and then we went home. In the subject that we did, we actually talked about what we as individuals thought. We gained experience from yourself and other people in the class and basically talked through for the two hours on the topics . . . in the other class the students at the front talked about what was in the book which we could read ourselves. We didn't need that so that was pointless. (Peter).

For Peter, the fact that the role of lecturer was now being played by the third-year students themselves made no qualitative difference to the interaction in the group. What emerges strongly is the need for dialogue, not monologue, as the dominant pedagogy. The power of this dialogic mode of inquiry to inform and to transform pre-service teachers is attested to by the participants themselves:

That was a really positive because I was starting to lose hope. . . . There's such an emphasis now on team work. (Vera)

It's been much better . . . because we're a bit more able to share information. . . . The interviews ended up being very easy. (Trevor)

Yeah, this [has] been great; yeah, I've really enjoyed it and I think probably because now that we're talking about pre-service teaching, we can relate to our prac . . . I can relate to this now and it means something and it's useful and it's going to be helpful next year. . . . Because we know what's worrying us about next year . . . it's being able to decide. . . . I just found it really wonderful . . . it was great. (Rosemarie)

Just like in-service . . . all the students have been saying that's
a really good idea and they've been writing them down. . . .
People are interacting in a way that's much more equal and
you know that you're focusing on the same things. . . . I've
really enjoyed that and I know everyone else has as well because I've come away with things that, y'know, are tangible
. . . that I can use, actually use and implement. (Andrea)

I tell people, "You should be in [our] class. We sit there and
talk but we all listen and all talk. We all contribute." (Dee)

Everything's coming together. . . . I guess I'm more aware of
teaching . . . it's a difficult world to save. . . but I think I can
make a difference there. (Marilyn)

Actually doing what we've done has made us different
people. . . . I don't think we were different necessarily to start
with . . . and I think I can see all of us in the group going
out and being more powerful teachers because of what we've
done. (Rita)

As a teacher educator, I learned a great deal about my own work as a
result of this. I have been confronted by the problems of long-term
critique and construct in piecemeal programs. I have realized how
much more work is involved in doing teacher education than in lecturing, seminar work, and practicum supervision. I have seen how readily
students will accept an academic's version of the truth on the one hand
and yet disdain it on the other. I have established on-going friendships
with my students. And I have discovered how much more I have to do
to provide my own in-service course in initial teacher education.

CHAPTER 6

POSTSCRIPT
Re-presenting Broken Images

FIRST-YEAR OU(S)T

Of the 14 research participants who contributed so much to my own education in teacher education, only 6 had entered the teaching profession within a year of completing their course. All but one of the others went on to further study in education, hoping that teaching employment opportunities would improve in the interim. They have not.

Rita, Mandy, Vera, and Melanie all gained immediate tenured employment in the state education department. For Rita, this was to mean service in the western rural-urban fringe where unemployment and truancy were high, and resources and motivation low. Rita's optimism and natural ebullience were sorely tested. Her initial contact with the school was so deflating that she felt compelled to ask, at the initial staff meeting, "Is there anyone who would like to tell me anything *good* that happens here? So far all I've heard is the bad and the ugly." Still, she was determined to do more than "glorified child-minding" and developed some very innovative programs at the risk of her own health and personal relationships. Her colleagues seemed to her at times to be more jealous than supportive of her success. Having told her how little was possible given the "sort of clientele" at her school, it seemed that her own innovative success and popularity stood in opposition to "the possible" as collectively understood in the school. Rita has since moved to tutoring in Aboriginal and Islander Studies.

Vera, Melanie, and Mandy were all appointed to schools servicing more prosperous communities and, while all three were stressed by the initial workloads and responsibilities, only Mandy has since resigned and this because of an appointment to a remote town only days after her wedding. In my own estimation, Vera's and Mandy's success was to be somewhat expected, given their high energy, strong presence, and genuine delight in pedagogical work. However, I was very pleased to find Melanie, who had always been rather ambivalent about a career she had "drifted into," now so full of enthusiasm for her work. "I am meeting a real need here," she wrote after some months of service, "and I am challenged to use my expertise in creating language programs across the entire region."

Trevor, Margaret, Andrea, Peter, Dee, and Roxanne all continued their educational studies in order to "upgrade" their teaching diploma to a degree. This involved a further year of study, after which Trevor, Margaret, and Andrea eventually became full-time teachers with the Queensland Department of Education. Peter is now working with a great deal of commitment and enthusiasm for the AIDS Council. Dee continued to be deeply troubled by the thought of doing educational work in contemporary school cultures. Her negative practicum experience continued to haunt her, and she wrote depressingly of her options:

> I didn't want to come back to Uni, but a lot of people either bribed, coaxed, persuaded or demanded I go back, so here I am. I guess I'll finish the year but I really can't see myself continuing with Education for a while . . . who knows.

Dee currently works in a large department store in Brisbane and is, as she puts it, "bored out of [her] brain." Roxanne's taste for educational scholarship has seen her move on to Masters degree work. Creative, perceptive, and capable, she has already set her sights on an academic career and has begun to attend professional conferences and to publish in the area of language and media.

Neither John nor Marilyn wished to continue their studies and both were very keen to begin teaching. Marilyn eventually was offered some classroom supply work in a remote country area. A contract followed and she is now, though untenured, a full-time classroom teacher. John was very industrious in pursuing teaching options. His efforts took him to Narita, Japan, where he went to find work. He is now employed by an English academy in Nagoya and is very happy in his work, despite the fact that he continues to struggle with the mysteries of the Japanese language.

Of the entire group, only Ken left education altogether, his failure in the practicum having moved him to reconsider teaching as a profession. He is now completing nursing studies at another university, while working part-time in a day-care center for the aged. This is giving him a sense of success and self-efficacy he never knew in classroom teaching. I am pleased to note this shift, because pedagogies of possibility do more than broaden options in the classroom. They ought to allow more informed decisions about the role pedagogy might play in a host of possible futures. The most important result of a teacher education program may be, for any individual, an informed decision not to teach at all.

WHAT LESSONS FOR THE TEACHER EDUCATOR?

No teacher educator can ever hope to participate unproblematically in research projects about her students or in pedagogical projects with and for her students. As I moved to erase the lines of demarcation between critical pedagogy and advocacy research, I was forced to confront the fact that, as a teacher educator and researcher, I am always implicated in the very structures I am trying to change (Ellsworth, 1989, p. 310). The call of feminists to "counter-disciplinary practices in educational inquiry" (Lather, 1991b, p. 163) is made out of acknowledgment of this very problem. I have learned that contemporary feminist theorizing can be usefully applied to actual practices across a range of teacher education endeavors, from policy analysis to pedagogy and from research to the "reality" of field experiences. For me as a learner, this meant overcoming an initial fear of engaging with new vocabularies generated out of poststructuralist and postmodernist literature, which often seemed unnecessarily tentative and tenuous or too complex and clever. The unacceptable alternative was to work within a research culture in which pre-service teachers have been for the most part "captives" (Tisher & Wideen, 1990, p. 256) and in which academics have been largely the sole beneficiaries.

In focusing on student language in the discursive contexts in which it is generated, I have sought to generate new debates for myself and others. The metaphorical constructions of teacher work that many pre-service teachers generate in their own talk about their needs have provided a rich source of data out of which it has been possible to generate new metaphors that transcend a totalizing articulation of teacher education as liberal or conservative. The more compelling issue for teacher educators is how possibilities are either opened up or shut down by our own discursive practices framed by our social relations. This will be more fruitful than the application of labels that cannot account for the complexity of student language or the range of experiences students bring to their professional work.

In attempting to enact a politics of engagement with my own students as pre-service teachers, I have been challenged to confront the task of "prizing apart" the meanings and assumptions fused together in the stories I have generated about myself and them. This has meant, by implication, the abandonment of attempts to *re*present the objects of my teacher education investigations as if I had captured a reality independent of my representational apparatus (Lather, 1991a, p. 11). My attempt to deconstruct a taken-for-granted world in which both I and my students are constituted as subjects is for the purposes of finding not a "new objectivity" or a more lofty vantage point, but, in Lather's terms, "a more hesitant and partial scholarship" (p. 15). The metaphor of trying to "pin down and probe" pre-service teachers as the objects of my inquiry must give way to metaphorical language for telling open, partial, and relational stories. The point is not to capture the elusiveness and precariousness of our subjectivities but to develop ways to acknowledge this transience more fully. Narratives produced out of this type of endeavor are much more likely to help students to confront their own "subjugated knowledges" (Ellsworth, 1989, p. 309).

In doing *postpositivist* teacher education research, I have reconceptualized my critical objective. It no longer seems appropriate to understand my goal as seeking to overcome student resistance to "emancipatory" pedagogy. The issue is how to overcome my own resistance to the assumption that "their problem" has to do with not accepting my version of reality (Lather, 1989, p. 24). This means acknowledging pre-service teacher talk as a legitimate response to the relations of power/knowledge available to them as subjects of academic, professional, and policy discourses. It also requires suspending such value judgments as lamenting the apolitical cynicism of the graduate teacher, or the apolitical romantic individualism of the first-year student.

Research centered by either holism or dialectical resolution is inappropriate to the reflexivity teacher educators now need. Yet reflexive investigations into social subjectivities in teacher education are not as easy to accomplish in practice as to declare in intent. What I can identify so readily as folklore, myth, or ideology in the beliefs and assumptions of others has the appearance of "truth" for me. What I felt I had "intuited" out of our own teaching and learning experiences, or what prevailing beliefs there are about the "scientifically proven" nature of teacher education—these assumptions are not rendered up easily for scrutiny.

Inquiry into the struggle over teacher education discourse cannot proceed from any methodology that claims to be innocent in the sense of being neutral or foundational. This only means a conventional reshuffle of the same deck of cards without changing the rules or objectives of the academic game (Shaker & Ullrich, 1987, p. 14). The challenge is to change the objectives, the deck and the rules, by bringing to bear perspectives that are new, coherent, and accessible, a deliberate break with the frames in which research "findings" have been made in the past. Schön (1987) makes the point that framing knowledge differently leads researchers to "pay attention to different facts and to make different sense of the facts they notice" (p. 5). Framing research problems of teacher "socialization" and pre-service curriculum out of new feminist theory allows for a greater complexity in the forms that the "data" can take. It also allows, indeed demands, reflection on how the researcher's own pedagogy contributed to the meanings pre-service teachers were giving to their learning and teaching.

Pre-service teachers need to experience the research process in ways that allow them to articulate and reflect on their personal versions of teaching rather than merely imitating the articulations of others. It could be argued that the well-documented phenomenon of "reality shock" (Corcoran, 1981) experienced by beginning teachers is the shock of finding oneself dressed in borrowed garb that is more rhetoric than substance, regardless of ideological orientation. Meanwhile the struggle over whose disciplinary offerings are more "relevant" to pre-service teachers goes on. "Progressive" teachers who give boring monologic lectures on equity and who attempt to "deliver" social justice are as implicated in this state of affairs as their mainstream counterparts.

As academic teachers, we need to develop more powerful pedagogical tools, by embarking on research that is educative for our students and other teachers as well as for ourselves. This work must be documented to overcome the fears of critical pedagogues that reciprocity and negotiation with students ends with a narrow functionalism swamping the teacher education agenda.

I have argued that, when students enter into their teacher education course, their language contains discursive elements that are potentially powerful political notions of teaching. Their language also contains technocratic, therapeutic, individualistic, and other diverse discursive elements. These "student-centered" concerns for dialogic models of classroom engagement have been termed in the literature "idealistic," conflated with an apolitical language of humanistic psychology, elements of which are to be found in the sort of "individual therapy talk" that now permeates so many linguistic sites in western culture. Attitudinal research into "what student teachers think" has not differentiated an embryonic politicized and politicizing language from what might be termed "romantic individualism." Instead, much is made of a general "humanistic" orientation that gives way to the "realism" of "actual" teaching, either in the final stages of the course itself or in the first year of classroom teaching (Hoy, 1969; Hoy & Rees, 1977; Morrison & MacIntyre, 1969).

While these simplistic depictions of "student attitudes" have been attacked (Hanson & Herrington, 1976; Lacey, 1977) and possibilities raised of contradictory data (e.g., "strategic fraud") (Petty & Hogben, 1980), they have congealed nevertheless into a "truism" of teacher socialization (Henry, Knight, Lingard, & Taylor, 1988, p. 25). This can be partly explained by the fact that the work challenging reductionist labeling has generally remained within a positivist framework, unable to cater to the complexity of studying language as *contexts* framed within broader network of discursive practices—disciplinary, institutional, and societal.

Feminist poststructuralist theorizing of the nature of language has allowed a less judgmental, more telling analysis of student talk. Fraser's (1989) theorizing of needs interpretations, when applied to the needs talk of pre-service teachers, allows analysis of versions of "talk" that is contextualized by the framework of the social relations of the interlocutors (p. 164). Rather than labeling student talk "naive," "unrealistic," or "technicist," pre-service language achieves a new legitimacy, not as the "truth" about professional needs, but as "stories" appropriately constituted out of, and resistant to, the narrative conventions and vocabularies available to these students as student/teachers. The notion that these stories are not "pure" but contain internal contradictions and struggles, articulated as they are through a plurality of competing ways of talking about teaching and learning, is more useful to the contemporary researcher than attitudinal labels would be.

Further, the teacher/researcher now has cause to reflect in an ongoing way on the role of her own "expert talk" as a linguistic contributor in this struggle. Recognizing the power of a variety of discourses of teacher education to saturate student oppositional language, has allowed me as a critical teacher educator to make strategic pedagogical interventions that are less defensive and less likely to wither on the vine of good intentions. I have been able to be more responsive to my students' capacity to generate their own alternative vocabularies and to challenge expert discourses, rather than presuming that I can and ought to superimpose my own "on their behalf." Moreover, the co-theorizing of the research participants has allowed me to better understand the relationship between the construction of their "versions" of teacher needs and the program of teacher preparation in which they have been engaged. I have been forced to acknowledge the complicity of socially critical teacher educators in disabling future teachers. It is not only technocratic models that are guilty of inappropriate simplification and reductionism. Critical teacher educators must do more than provide and reiterate an ideal of the change-enhancing teacher. Our own research and teaching must give closer and more meticulous attention to practical means by which to become one.

To extend the possibilities for its clients, teacher education must move on from a model based on the simple, the single, and the separate, to one based on the complex, the incomplete, and the connected. This requires new texts formed out of new vocabularies. In postmodern times, teacher educators are challenged to adopt "a new dialogue with nature" and "a new relationship with our students, a radically new relationship" (Doll, 1989, p. 248). A new dialogue will not be forthcoming while we continue to work "quick and dull" out of old oppositions and traditional modes of representation.

The tales told in this book have all been attempts to *re*-present my own teacher education work and that of others, working "slow and sharp" by drawing on feminist debates within and against poststructuralism and postmodernism. I have used neo-feminist strategies to unsettle binary formulations (theory/practice; idealism/realism; humanistic/custodial; dominant/avant-garde; progressive/conservative) that still pervade teacher educators' descriptions of how teacher competence is acquired. These binary systems invented in the writing of teacher education research constrain exploration of appropriate and necessary connections across isolated areas of endeavor in the teacher education project. New feminist theorizing is not the "solution." But, given what new feminist theories offer, we can now hope for more telling tales.

NOTES

Chapter 1

1. See, for example, Knight, J., Bartlett, L., and McWilliam, E. (Eds.). (1993). *Unfinished Business: Reshaping the Teacher Education Industry for the 1990's.* Rockhampton: University of Central Queensland Press.

Chapter 2

1. Roland Barthes (1973, p. 117) uses this phrase when speaking of the ability of certain sorts of discourse to gain the status of myth consumed as fact rather than as a complex semiological system of values.

2. In her use of this term, Gore is drawing on the work of Michel Foucault, whose notion of a "regime" or "general politics" of truth was alluded to in Chapter 1.

3. See Sewell's (1992) critique of the work of both Giddens and Bourdieu, *A Theory of Structure: Duality, Agency and Transformation.* He argues that "structure" is "one of the most important, elusive and undertheorized concepts in the social sciences" (p. 1).

4. As I have argued elsewhere (McWilliam, 1987), this term is misleading because it suggests a coherent and consistent ideological movement. The one-dimensional clarity of linear metaphors like "left" as distinct from "right" is made problematic in poststructuralist analysis.

5. This term is used to distinguish the work of contemporary feminists of the 1980s and 1990s from earlier feminist work. What women have in common with men was stressed in the demand for "equality with men" by means of "an equal share of social benefit" in feminisms of egalitarianism of the 1960s and 1970s. However, contemporary feminists see the need to assert different agendas more strongly in order to signal appropriate historical shifts in demanding women's rights.

6. The problems faced by feminists in engaging with postmodern notions is a vast topic in itself. Feminist writings in Nicholson, L. (Ed.). (1990).

Feminism/Postmodernism are a useful entrée into the dilemmas alluded to here. It is clear that these feminists have taken no unified stance regarding the value of postmodernist/poststructuralist ideas.

Chapter 3

1. The reader will be relieved to know that the munching metaphor will not be extended throughout, Michael Apple having already been referred to in a previous chapter.

2. Saussure's classical structuralist work made the distinction between *language* (langue) and *word* (parole) without acknowledging the problems of translation within one and the same language. Pecheux noted the importance of the relation between changes in the meanings of words and the positions held by those who employ them. See Thompson (1984, pp. 232–254), Chapter 7, "Ideology and the Analysis of Discourse: A Critical Introduction to the Work of Michel Pecheux."

Chapter 4

1. The names used for all the research participants are pseudonyms.

2. This theme emerged more strongly for Ken as his course proceeded. He was failed in his final practicum and gave up on a teaching career altogether. He is now experiencing more success in a career in nursing.

3. An analysis of Australia's employment patterns in the next decade, for example, saw psychology as having the most potential for growth of any occupation (93 %) (*The Courier Mail*, September 28, 1991).

Chapter 5

1. McTaggart's (1991b) *Action Research: A Short Modern History* provides a recent and useful overview of the range of studies termed "action research." It is clear that an explicitly socially critical dimension has been a recent historical development.

2. This politics was to some extent played out in the ecological setting of the room, as students tended to form an arc separate from me, despite my creating a circle of chairs at the outset. This was most evident in the Wednesday group, which seemed more content with the role of "discipleship" at the outset, than the Friday group. As the research progressed, I was pleased to note that the ecological focus of the room changed in both classes. Students recreated the circle of chairs we had commenced with.

3. This is the term Glasser (1969) uses, and it is appropriately nonjudgmental in a discussion of classroom disruption. I found that, in using it in my own work as a secondary school teacher, I was less likely to "blame the victim" and more likely to focus on putting an end to the disruption.

REFERENCES

Althusser, L. (1971). Ideology and ideological state apparatuses. In L. Althusser (Ed.), *Lenin and philosophy and other essays* (pp. 127–186). New York: Monthly Review Press.

Apple, M. (1979). *Ideology and curriculum.* New York: Routledge and Kegan Paul.

Apple, M. (1988). *Teachers and texts: A political economy of class and gender relations in education.* New York: Routledge and Kegan Paul.

Applegate, J. (1987). Early field experiences: Three viewpoints. In M. Haberman & J. Backus (Eds.), *Advances in teacher education, Volume 3* (pp. 75–91). Norwood, NJ: Ablex.

Armaline, W., & Hoover, R. (1989). Field experience as a vehicle for transformation: Ideology, education and reflective practice. *Journal of Teacher Education, 40*(2), 42–48.

Atkinson, P., & Delamont, S. (1985). Socialization into teaching: The research which lost its way. *British Journal of Sociology of Education, 6*(3), 307–322.

Austin, J. (1976). *How to do things with words.* Oxford: Oxford University Press.

Australian Education Council. (1990). *Teacher education in Australia: Report to the Australian Education Council* (The Ebbeck Report). Melbourne: AEC.

Australian Education Council Review Committee. (1991). *Young people's participation in post-compulsory education and training* (The Finn Report). Canberra: AGPS

Ball, S. (1990). Introducing Monsieur Foucault. In S. Ball (Ed.), *Foucault and education: Disciplines and knowledge* (pp. 1–7). New York: Routledge and Kegan Paul.

Ball, S. (1993). What is policy: Texts, trajectories and toolboxes. *Discourse: The Australian Journal of Educational Studies, 13*(2), 10–17.

Bannister, D. (1981). Personal construct theory and research method. In P. Reason & J. Rowan (Eds.), *Human inquiry* (pp. 191–199). London: John Wiley and Sons.

Barrow, R. (1984). *Giving teaching back to teachers: A critical introduction to curriculum theory.* Sussex: Wheatsheaf Books.

Barthes, R. (1973). *Mythologies.* London: Granada.

Bartlett, L. (1989, March). *A question of good judgement: Interpretation theory and qualitative inquiry.* Paper presented at the annual meeting of the American Educational Research Association, San Francisco.

Bartlett, L. (1990). *Defining the qualitative in hermeneutic educational research.* Unpublished manuscript. University of Queensland.

Bartlett, L. (1991, July). *Competency-based standards in the professions in Australia: Implications and applications for the teaching profession.* Paper presented at the twenty-first annual conference of the Australian Teacher Education Association, Melbourne.

Bartlett, L., Knight, J., & Lingard, R. (1991). Corporate federalism and the reform of teacher education in Australia. *Journal of Education Policy, 6*(1), 91–95.

Bates, R. (1992, November). *Educational reform: Its role in the destruction of society.* Keynote address, Joint AARE/NZARE Annual Conference, Deakin University Geelong.

Battersby, D. (1986, March). *A review of research on beginning teachers and teacher socialisation.* (Occasional Paper 4). Education Department, Massey University.

Battersby, D., & Ramsay, P. (1983). Professional socialization of teachers: Towards improved methodology. *New Education, 5*(1), 77–84.

Battersby, D., & Ramsay, P. (1990). Practice teaching in New Zealand. *South Pacific Journal of Teacher Education, 18*(1), 19–26.

Battersby, D., & Retallick, J. (1988). The discourse of teacher education policy in Australia. *Australian Journal of Teacher Education, 13*(1 & 2), 9–13.

Beauchamp, L., & Parsons, J. (1989). The curriculum of student teacher evaluation. *Journal of Curriculum Theorising, 9*(1), 125–171.

Benhabib, S. (1990). Epistemologies of postmodernism: A rejoinder to Jean-François Lyotard. In L. Nicholson (Ed.), *Feminism/postmodernism* (pp. 107–130). New York: Routledge and Kegan Paul.

Bennison, A., Jungck, S., Kantor, K., & Marshall, D. (1989). Teachers' voices in curriculum inquiry: A conversion among teacher educators. *Journal of Curriculum Theorizing, 9*(1), 71–105.

Bernstein, B. (1986). On pedagogic discourse. In J. Richardson (Ed.), *Handbook of theory and research in the sociology of education* (pp. 205–240). Westport, CT: Greenwood Press.

Bernstein, R. (1983). *Beyond objectivism and relativism: Science, hermeneutics and praxis.* Philadelphia: University of Pennsylvania Press.

Bertaux, D., & Kohli, M. (1984). The life story approach: A continental view. *Annual Review of Sociology, 10*, 215–237.

Beyer, B. (1979). *Teaching thinking in social studies.* Columbus, OH: Merrill.

Beyer, B. (1984a). Improving thinking skills—Defining the problem. *Phi Delta Kappan, 65*(7), 486–490.

Beyer, B. (1984b). Improving thinking skills—Practical approaches. *Phi Delta Kappan, 65*(8), 556–560.

Beyer, L. (1988). *Knowing and acting: Inquiry, ideology and educational studies.* London: The Falmer Press.

Beyer, L., & Zeichner, K. (1981, April). Teacher education in cultural context: Moving beyond reproduction. Paper presented at the annual meeting of the American Educational Research Association, Los Angeles.

Borthwick, J. (1986, November). *Interpreting the experience of pre-service teacher education: Theory, structure and action in education.* Paper presented at the annual conference of the Australian Association for Research in Education, Ormond College, University of Melbourne.

Bourne, G. (1981). Meaning, image and ideology. In G. Martin, G. Bourne, J. Donald, & C. Mercer (Eds.), *Form and meaning 1, popular culture* (pp. 38–65). Milton Keynes, England: The Open University Press.

Bowe, R., Ball, S., & Gold, A. (1992). *Reforming education and changing schools: Case studies in policy sociology.* London: Routledge and Kegan Paul.

Bowles, S., & Gintis, H. (1976). *Schooling in capitalist America.* New York: Basic Books.

Boynton, P., Di Geronimo, J., & Gustafson, G. (1985). A basic survival guide for new teachers. *The Clearing House, 59*(3), 101–103.

Brooks, D. (1985). The teacher's communicative competence: The first day of school. *Theory into Practice, 34*(1), 63–70.

Buckingham, B. (1926). *Research for teachers.* New York: Silver, Burdett.

Bullough, R. (1987). Planning and the first year of teaching. *Journal of Education for Teaching, 13*(3), 50–68.

Cairns, L. (1992). Competency-based education: Nostradamus's nostrum? *Journal of Teaching Practice, 12*(1), 1–32.

Caputo, J. (1987). *Radical hermeneutics: Repetition, reconstruction and the hermeneutic project.* Bloomington: Indiana University Press.

Carmichael, L. (1992). *The Australian vocational certificate training system.* Canberra: NBEET.

Carnegie Forum on Education and the Economy. (1986). *A nation prepared: Teachers for the twenty-first century.* New York: Carnegie Corporation.

Carr, W. (1980). The gap between theory and practice. *Journal of Further and Higher Education, 4*(1), 60–69.

Carr, W. (1989). Introduction: Understanding quality in teaching. In W. Carr (Ed.), *Quality in teaching: Arguments for a reflective profession* (pp. 1–20). London: The Falmer Press.

Carr, W., & Kemmis, S. (1986). *Becoming critical: Education, knowledge and action research.* London: The Falmer Press.

Cheney, L. (Chairperson). (1987). *American memory: A report on the humanities in the nation's public schools.* Washington DC: National Endowment for the Humanities.

Connell, R. (1985). *Teachers' work.* Sydney: George Allen and Unwin.

Connor, S. (1989). *Postmodernist culture: An introduction to theories of the contemporary.* Oxford: Basil Blackwell.

Corcoran, E. (1981). Transition shock: The beginning teacher's paradox. *Journal of Teacher Education, 32*(3), 19–23.

Corey, S. (1953). *Action research to improve school practices.* New York: Teachers College Press.

Cruickshank, D., & Applegate, T. (1981). Reflective teaching as a strategy for teacher growth. *Educational Leadership, 38*(7), 553–554.

Curthoys, A. (1988). Culture and politics; or the shibboleths of the left. In L. Grossberg, T. Fry, A. Curthoys, & P. Patton (Eds.), *It's a sin: Essays on postmodernism, politics and culture* (pp. 83–87). Sydney: Power Publications.

Dale, R. (1977). *The structural context of teaching.* Milton Keynes, England: The Open University Press.

Davies, B. (1987, August). *The sense children make of feminist fairy stories.* Paper presented at the South World Congress of Applied Linguistics, University of Sydney.

Deal, T., & Chatman, R. (1989). Learning the ropes alone: Socialising new teachers. *Action in Teacher Education, 11*(1), 21–29.

den Hartog, D., & Alomes, S. (1991). Introduction: From popular culture to cultural studies—and beyond. In S. Alomes & D. den Hartog (Eds.), *Post pop: Popular culture, nationalism and postmodernism* (pp. 1–26). Melbourne, Victoria University of Technology: Footprint.

Denscombe, M. (1982). The "hidden pedagogy" and its implications for teacher training. *British Journal of Sociology of Education, 3*(3), 249–265.

Denscombe, M. (1985). *Classroom control: A sociological perspective.* London: George Allen and Unwin.

Department of Education and Science. (1983). *Teacher quality* (Cmnd 8836). London: HMSO.

Department of Employment, Education and Training. (1989). *Discipline review of teacher education in mathematics and science.* Canberra: Australian Government Printing Service.

Derrida, J. (1970). Structure, sign and play in the discourse of the human sciences. In R. Macksey & E. Donato (Eds.), *The languages of criticism and the sciences of man: The structuralist controversy* (pp. 247–272). Baltimore: Johns Hopkins University Press.

Diamond, C. (1988). Construing a career: A developmental view of teacher education and the teacher educator. *Journal of Curriculum Studies, 20*(2), 133–140.

Di Stephano, C. (1990). Dilemmas of difference: Feminism, modernity and postmodernism. In L. Nicholson (Ed.), *Feminism/postmodernism* (pp. 63–82). New York: Routledge and Kegan Paul.

Doll, W. (1989). Foundations for a post-modern curriculum. *Journal of Curriculum Studies, 21*(3), 243–253.

Eco, U. (1986). *Faith in fakes: Essays* (William Weaver, Trans.). London: Secker and Warburg.

Eisner, E. (1983). Anastasia might be alive but the monarchy is dead. *Educational Researcher, 12*(5), 13–24.

Eisner, E. (1988). The primacy of experience and the politics of method. *Educational Researcher, 17*(5), 15–20.

Elbaz, F. (1988). Critical reflection on teaching: Insights from Freire. *Journal of Teacher Education, 40*(2), 171–181.

Elliot, J. (1988). Educational research and outsider-insider relations. *International Journal of Qualitative Studies in Education, 1*(2), 54–62.

Ellsworth, E. (1989). Why doesn't this feel empowering: Working through the repressive myths of critical pedagogy. *Harvard Educational Review, 59*(3), 297–324.

Everton, C., Hawley, W., & Zlotnik, M. (1984). *The characteristics of effective teacher education programmes: A review of research.* Nashville: Peabody College, Nashville University.

Fay, B. (1977). How people change themselves: The relationship between critical theory and its audience. In T. Ball (Ed.), *Political theory and praxis* (pp. 200–233). Minneapolis: University of Minnesota Press.

Feldman, K. (1972). Some theoretical approaches to the study of change and stability of college students. *Review of Educational Research, 42,* 1–26.

Foucault, M. (1972/1977). *The archeology of knowledge.* London: Tavistock.

Foucault, M. (1980). *Power/knowledge: Selected interviews and other writings 1972–1977.* New York: Pantheon.

Foucault, M. (1981). Questions of method: An interview with Michel Foucault. *Ideology and Consciousness, 8,* 3–14.

Foucault, M. (1982). Afterword: The subject and power. In H. Dreyfus & P. Rabinow (Eds.), *Michel Foucault: Beyond structuralism and hermeneutics* (pp. 208–228). Brighton, England: Harvester Press.

Fraser, N. (1989). *Unruly practices: Power, discourse and gender in contemporary social theory.* Cambridge: Polity Press.

Freire, P. (1973). *Pedagogy of the oppressed.* New York: Seabury Press.

Freire, P. (1985). *The politics of education: Culture, power and liberation.* South Hadley, MA: Bergen and Garvey.

Fuller, F. (1969). Concerns for teachers: A developmental conceptualization. *American Educational Research Journal, 6,* 207–226.

Gadamer, H. (1975). *Truth and method* (G. Barden & J. Cumming, Eds. & Trans.). New York: Seabury Press.

Geertz, C. (1973). *The interpretation of cultures.* New York: Basic Books.

Gehrke, N., & Yamamoto, K. (1978, April). *A grounded theory study of the role personalisation of beginning secondary teachers.* Paper presented at the annual meeting of the American Educational Research Association, Toronto.

Giddens, A. (1976). *New rules of sociological method.* London: Heinemann.

Giddens, A., & Turner, J. (1987). *Social theory today.* Cambridge: Polity Press.

Gill, G. (1991). The social origins of postmodernism. In S. Alomes & D. den Hartog (Eds.), *Post pop: Popular culture, nationalism and postmodernism* (pp. 38–45). Melbourne, Victoria University of Technology: Footprint.

Ginsburg, M. (1988). *Contradictions in teacher education and society.* London: The Falmer Press.

Ginsberg, M., & Newman, K. (1981, April). *Socialisation of pre-service teachers and the reproduction/transformation of society.* Paper presented at the annual meeting of the American Educational Research Association, Los Angeles.

Giroux, H. (1981). *Ideology, culture and the process of schooling*. London: The Falmer Press.

Giroux, H. (1983). *Theory and resistance in education*. South Hadley, MA: Bergin and Garvey.

Giroux, H. (1991). Border pedagogy and the politics of postmodernism. *Social Text, 9*(3), 51–67.

Gitlin, A., Siegel, M., & Boru, K. (1988, April). *Purpose and method: Rethinking the use of ethnography by the educational left*. Paper presented at the annual meeting of the American Educational Research Association, San Francisco.

Glasser, W. (1969). *Schools without failure*. New York: Harper and Row.

Goodman, J. (1986, April). *Constructing a practical philosophy of teaching: A study of preservice teachers' professional perspectives*. Paper presented at the annual meeting of the American Educational Research Association, San Francisco.

Goodman, J., & Adler, S. (1985). Becoming an elementary social studies teacher: A study of perspectives. *Theory and Research in Education, 13*(2), 1–20.

Gordon, B. (1985). Teaching teachers: "Nation at risk" and the issue of knowledge in teacher education. *The Urban Review, 17*(1), 33–46.

Gore, J. (1987). Reflecting on reflective teaching. *Journal of Teacher Education, 38*(2), 33–39.

Gore, J. (1991). On silent regulation: Emancipatory action research in preservice teacher education. *Curriculum Perspectives, 11*(4), 47–51.

Gore, J. (1993). *The struggle for pedagogies: Critical and feminist discourses as regimes of truth*. New York: Routledge and Kegan Paul.

Gottlieb, E. (1989). The discursive construction of knowledge: The case of radical education discourse. *Qualitative Studies in Education, 2*(2), 131–144.

Graff, G. (1988). Foreward. In J. Herron, *Universities and the myth of cultural decline* (pp. 9–19). Detroit: Wayne State University Press.

Grant, C., & Sleeter, C. (1985). Who determines teacher work: The teacher, the organisation or both? *Teaching and Teacher Education, 1*(3), 209–220.

Greene, M. (1993). Reflections on postmodernism and education. *Educational Policy, 7*(2), 206–211.

Grosz, E. (1990). Contemporary theories of power and subjectivity. In S. Gunew (Ed.), *Feminist knowledge: Critique and construct* (pp. 59–120). New York: Routledge and Kegan Paul.

Grumet, M. (1989a). Generations: Reconceptualist curriculum theory and teacher education. *Journal of Teacher Education, 40*(1), 13–17.

Grumet, M. (1989b). Word worlds: The literary reference for curriculum criticism. *Journal of Curriculum Theorising, 9*(1), 7–21.

Gunew, S. (Ed.). (1990). *Feminist knowledge: Critique and construct*. New York: Routledge and Kegan Paul.

Hall, S. (1979, January). The great moving right show. *Marxism Today*, 11–20.

Halliday, M., & Hasan, R. (1985). *Language, context, and text: Aspects of language in a social-semiotic perspective*. Geelong: Deakin University Press.

Hanson, D., & Herrington, M. (1976). *From college to classroom*. New York: Routledge and Kegan Paul.

Harding, S. (1986). *The science question in feminism*. Ithaca, NY: Cornell University Press.

Harding, S. (Ed.). (1987). *Feminism and methodology*. Bloomington: Indiana University Press.

Harding, S. (1990). Feminism, science and the anti-Enlightenment critiques. In L. Nicholson (Ed.), *Feminism/postmodernism* (pp. 83–106). New York: Routledge and Kegan Paul.

Hatton, E. (1989). Levi-Strauss' *Bricolage* and theorising teachers' work. *Anthropology and Education Quarterly, 20*(2), 74–96.

Hatton, E. (1991). Teachers' work and teacher education. *Discourse: The Australian Journal of Educational Studies, 12*(1), 124–139.

Hawley, W. (1992). United States. In H. Leavitt (Ed.), *Issues and problems in teacher education: An international handbook* (pp. 247–278). Westport, CT: Greenwood Press.

Hebdidge, D. (1988). *Hiding in the light: On images and things*. New York: Routledge and Kegan Paul.

Henderson, J. (1988). A curriculum response to the knowledge base reform movement. *Journal of Teacher Education, 39*(5), 13–17.

Henriques, J., Holloway, W., Urwin, C., Venn, C., & Walkerdine, V. (1984a). From the individual to the social—a bridge too far. In J. Henriques, W. Holloway, C. Urwin, C. Venn, & V. Walkerdine (Eds.), *Changing the subject: Psychology, social regulation and subjectivity* (pp. 11–25). London and New York: Methuen.

Henriques, J., Holloway, W., Urwin, C., Venn, C., & Walkerdine, V. (1984b). Introduction to Section 2: Constructing the subject. In J. Henriques, W. Holloway, C. Urwin, C. Venn, & V. Walkerdine (Eds.), *Changing the subject: Psychology, social regulation and subjectivity* (pp. 91–118). London and New York: Methuen.

Henry, M., Knight, J., Lingard, R., & Taylor, S. (1988). *Understanding schooling: An introductory sociology of Australian education*. New York: Routledge and Kegan Paul.

Hextall, I., Lawn, M., Menter, I., Sidgwick, S., & Walker, S. (1991). *Imaginative projects: Arguments for a new teacher education*. London: University of London, Faculty of Education.

Hill, D. (1990). *Something old, something new, something borrowed, something blue: Schooling, teacher education and the radical right in Britain and the USA* (Hillcole Group Paper 3). London: Tufnell Press.

Hirsch, E. (1987). *Cultural literacy: What every American needs to know*. Boston: Houghton-Mifflin.

Hodges, C. (1982). Implementing methods: If you can't blame the co-operating teacher, whom can you blame? *Journal of Teacher Education, 33*, 25–29.

Hogan, P. (1988). Communicative competence and cultural emancipation: Reviewing the rationale for educational studies in teacher education. *Oxford Review of Education, 14*(2), 187–200.

Hogben, D., & Lawson, M. (1983). Attitudes of secondary school trainees and their practice teaching supervisors. *Journal of Education for Teaching, 9*(3), 249–263.

Holloway, W. (1984). Fitting work: Psychological assessment in organisations. In J. Henriques, W. Holloway, C. Urwin, C. Venn, & V. Walkerdine (Eds.), *Changing the subject: Psychology, social regulation and subjectivity* (pp. 26–59). London and New York: Methuen.

Holmes Group. (1986). *Tomorrow's teachers: A report of the Holmes Group.* East Lansing, MI: Holmes Group.

hooks, b. (1989). *Talking back: Thinking feminist thinking black.* Boston: South End Press.

Howey, K., & Gardner, W. (1983). *A current profile of the American teacher: Some implications for international education.* Paper presented at the International Council on Education for Teaching, Washington, DC.

Hoy, W. (1969). Pupil control ideology and organisational socialisation: A further examination of the influences of experience on the beginning teacher. *School Review, 77,* 257–265.

Hoy, W., & Rees, R. (1977). The bureaucratic socialisation of student teachers. *Journal of Teacher Education, 28*(1), 23–26.

Hukill, H., & Hughes, G. (1983, April). *Teachers for tomorrow.* Paper presented at the annual meeting of the American Educational Research Association, Montreal.

Hunter, I. (1984). Laughter and warmth: Sex education in Victorian secondary schools. In P. Botsman and R. Harley (Eds.), *Sex, politics, representation* (pp. 55–118). Sydney: Local Consumption Publications.

Hunter, I. (1992). The humanities without humanism. *Meanjin, 3,* 479–490.

Irigaray, L. (1984). *L'ethique de la difference sexuelle.* Paris: Editions de Minuit.

Irigaray, L. (1985). *Speculum of the other woman.* Ithaca, NY: Cornell University Press.

Jamieson, I. (1989). Education and the economy: Themes and issues. *Journal of Education Policy, 4*(1), 69–73.

Jay, M. (1988). *Fin-de-siecle socialism and other essays.* New York: Routledge and Kegan Paul.

Jencks, C. (1979). *Who gets ahead?* New York: Basic Books.

Johnson, R. (1980). Cultural studies and education. *Screen, 34,* 5–16.

Joyce, B. (1978). A problem of categories: Classifying approaches to teaching. *Boston University Journal of Education, 160,* 67–95.

Katz, L., & Raths, J. (1982). The best of intentions for the education of teachers. *Action in Teacher Education, 4,* 8–16.

Kemmis, S. (1988, May). *Critical educational research.* A paper prepared for a meeting of the Critical Theory Preconference of the North American Adult Education Association Research Conference, University of Calgary.

Kemmis, S. (1991). Emancipatory action research and postmodernisms. *Curriculum Perspectives, 11*(4), 60–66.

Kemmis, S., & McTaggart, R. (1988). *The action research planner (3rd ed.).* Geelong: Deakin University Press.

Kiziltan, M., Bain, J., & Canizares, A. (1990). Postmodern conditions: Rethinking public education. *Educational Theory, 40*(3), 351–369.

Knight, J., McWilliam, E., & Bartlett, L. (1993). The road ahead: Refashioning Australian teacher education for the twenty-first century. In J. Knight, L. Bartlett, & E. McWilliam (Eds.), *Unfinished business: Reshaping the teacher education industry for the 1990s* (pp. 139–153). Rockhampton, Queensland: University of Central Queensland Press.

Korthagen, F. (1985). Reflective teaching and pre-service teacher education in the Netherlands. *Journal of Teacher Education, 36*(5), 11–15.

Lacey, C. (1977). *The socialization of teachers.* London: Methuen.

Laclau, E., & Mouffe, C. (1982). Re-casting Marxism: Hegemony and new political movements. *Socialist Review, 66*(6), 91–113.

Lather, P. (1986). Research as praxis. *Harvard Educational Review, 56*(3), 257–277.

Lather, P. (1988). Feminist perspectives on empowering research methodologies. *Women's Studies International Forum, 11*(6), 569–581.

Lather, P. (1989). *Deconstructing/deconstructive inquiry: Issues in feminist research methodologies.* Paper presented at the New Zealand Women's Studies Association Conference, Christchurch.

Lather, P. (1991a). *Feminist research in education: Within/against.* Geelong: Deakin University Press.

Lather, P. (1991b). Deconstructing/deconstructive inquiry: The politics of knowing and being known. *Educational Theory, 41*(2), 153–173.

Lather, P. (1993). Fertile obsession: Validity after poststructuralism. *Sociological Quarterly, 34*(4), 673–693.

Lauder, H., Middleton, S., Boston, J., & Wylie, C. (1988). The third wave: A critique of the New Zealand Treasury's report on education. *New Zealand Journal of Educational Studies, 23*(1), 15–34.

Lauglo, J. (1975). Teachers' social origins, career commitments during university and occupational attitudes. *Sociology of Education, 48*, 278–307.

Lawn, M., & Barton, L. (1985). Making sociologists confess. *British Journal of Sociology of Education, 6*(1), 117–121.

Lawton, D. (1984). *The tightening grip: Growth of central control of the school curriculum.* London: University of London Institute of Education.

Leggatt, T. (1970). Teaching as a profession. In J. Jackson (Ed.), *Professions and professionalisation* (pp. 153–178). London: Cambridge University Press.

Lemlech, J., & Kaplan, S. (1990). Learning to talk about teaching: Collegiality in clinical teacher education. *Action in Teacher Education, 12*(1), 13–19.

Lesko, N. (1988). *Symbolising society: Stories, rites and structure in a Catholic high school.* London: The Falmer Press.

Lewin, K. (1946). Action research and minority problems. *Journal of Social Issues, 2*, 34–46.

Lewis, M. (1990). Interrupting patriarchy: Politics, resistance, and transformation in the feminist classroom. *Harvard Educational Review, 60*(4), 467–489.

Lieberman, M. (1956). *Education as a profession.* Englewood Cliffs, NJ: Prentice-Hall.

Lingard, R. (1991). Policy-making for Australian schooling: The new corporate federalism. *Journal of Education Policy, 6*(1), 85–90.

Liston, D., & Zeichner, K. (1987, April). *Critical pedagogy and teacher education.* Paper presented at the annual meeting of the American Educational Research Association, New Orleans.

Lortie, D. (1975). *School teacher: A sociological study.* Chicago: University of Chicago Press.

Lusted, D. (1986). Why pedagogy? *Screen, 27*(5), 2–14.

MacIntyre, A. (1984). *After virtue: A study in moral theory.* South Bend, IN: University of Notre Dame Press.

Marginson, S. (1992, February). *Economic rationalism in education.* Paper presented at the "Rationalising Australia" Conference, Flinders University, South Australia.

Marshall, J. (1990). Foucault and educational research. In S. Ball (Ed.), *Foucault and education: Disciplines and knowledge* (pp. 11–28). New York: Routledge and Kegan Paul.

Maxie, A. (1989, March). *Student teachers' concerns and the student-teaching experience: Does experience make a difference?* Paper presented at the annual meeting of the American Educational Research Association, San Francisco.

Mayer Committee. (1992). *Employment-related key competencies: A proposal for consultation.* Melbourne: Mayer Committee.

Maynard, D. (1975). Personality characteristics of community college students. *Journal of College Student Personnel, 16,* 323–329.

McArthur, J. (1981). *The first five years of teaching.* Canberra: Australian Government Printing Service.

McLaren, P. (1986). *Schooling as ritual performance.* New York: Routledge and Kegan Paul.

McLaren, P. (1988). Language, structure and the language of subjectivity. *Critical Pedagogy Networker, 1*(2 & 3), 1–10.

McPherson, G. (1972). *Small town teacher.* Cambridge: Harvard University Press.

McTaggart, R. (1991a). Action research is a broad movement. *Curriculum Perspectives, 11*(4), 45–47.

McTaggart, R. (1991b). *Action research: A short modern history.* Geelong: Deakin University Press.

McWilliam, E. (1987). The challenge of the new right: It's liberty versus equality and to hell with fraternity. *Discourse: The Australian Journal of Educational Studies, 8*(1), 61–76.

McWilliam, E. (1992). *In broken images: A postpositivist analysis of student needs talk in pre-service teacher education.* Unpublished doctoral dissertation, University of Queensland, Department of Education.

McWilliam, E. (1993a). Post haste: Plodding research and galloping theory. *British Journal of Sociology of Education, 14*(1), 199–205.

McWilliam, E. (1993b). Thinking impure thoughts: Some concerns about critical pedagogy as "democratic" tertiary teaching. *Social Alternatives, 12*(2), 33–36.

Meighan, R. (1981). *A sociology of educating.* London: Holt, Rinehart and Winston.

Miller, S. (1990). Foucault on discourse and power. *Theoria, 76,* 115–125.

Mishler, E. (1990). Validation in inquiry-guided research: The role of exemplars in narrative studies. *Harvard Educational Review, 60*(4), 415–442.

Morrison, A., & MacIntyre, D. (1969). *Teachers and teaching* (2nd ed.). Harmondsworth: Penguin.

Munby, H., & Russell, T. (1989). Educating the reflective teacher: An essay review of two books by Donald Schön. *Journal of Curriculum Studies, 21*(1), 71–80.

Newton, E., & Brathwaite, W. (1987). Priorities and program effectiveness in teacher education: A study of the perceptions of teachers in training and their tutors. *Teaching and Teacher Education, 3*(3), 87.

Nicholson, L. (Ed.). (1990). *Feminism/postmodernism.* New York: Routledge and Kegan Paul.

Noffke, S. (1991). Hearing the teacher's voice: Now what? *Curriculum Perspectives, 11*(4), 55–59.

O'Loughlin, M., & Campbell, M. (1988). Teacher preparation, teacher empowerment and reflective inquiry: A critical perspective. *Education and Society, 6*(1 & 2), 54–70.

Orner, M., & Brennan, M. (1989, March). *Producing collectively: Power, identity and teaching.* A paper produced for presentation in the inaugural Special Interest Group "Media, Culture and Curriculum" at the annual meeting of the American Educational Research Association, San Francisco.

Paine, L. (1990). *Orientation towards diversity: What do prospective teachers bring?* East Lansing, MI: National Center for Research on Teacher Education.

Palonsky, S., & Jacobson, M. (1989). Student teacher perceptions of elementary school social studies: The social construction of curriculum. *Journal of Social Studies Research, 13*(1), 28–33.

Patai, D. (1988). Constructing a self: A Brazilian life story. *Feminist Studies, 14*(1), 143–166.

Pecheux, M. (1975). *Les verites de la palice: Linguistique, semantique, philosophie.* Paris: Maspero.

Peters, M., & Marshall, J. (1989). *Education, the "new right" and the crisis of the welfare state in New Zealand.* Unpublished manuscript, University of Auckland.

Petty, M., & Hogben, D. (1980). Explorations of semantic space with beginning teachers: A study of socialisation into teaching. *British Journal of Teacher Education, 6,* 51–61.

Plowden Report, The. (1967). *Children and their primary schools.* Central Advisory Council for Education: HMSO

Popkewitz, T. (1979, April). *Teacher education as socialization: Ideology or social mission.* Paper presented at the annual meeting of the American Educational Research Association, San Francisco.

Popkewitz, T. (1985). Ideology and social formation in teacher education. *Teaching and Teacher Education, 1*(2), 91–107.

Popkewitz, T. (Ed.). (1987). *Critical studies in teacher education: Its folklore, theory and practice.* London: The Falmer Press.

Porter, P. (1990, July). *Keynote Address.* Abel Smith Lecture Theatre, University of Queensland.

Porter, P., Lingard, R., & Knight, J. (1991). *Restructuring for better schools in Western Australia.* Paper presented at the annual conference of the Australian Association for Research in Education, Surfers Paradise, Queensland.

Poster, N. (1989). *Critical theory and poststructuralism: In search of a context.* London: Cornell.

Price, D. (1989). The practicum: A recent review of the literature. *The South Pacific Journal of Teacher Education, 17*(2), 13–23.

Rabinow, P., & Sullivan, W. (Eds.). (1979). *Interpretive social science.* Berkeley: University of California Press.

Reason, P., & Rowan, J. (1981). Issues of validity in new paradigm research. In P. Reason & J. Rowan (Eds.), *Human inquiry* (pp. 239–252). New York: Wiley.

Roman, L. (1993). Raymond William's unfinished project: The articulation of a socially transformative critical realism. *Discourse: The Australian Journal of Educational Studies, 13*(2), 18–34.

Romanish, B. (1987). A skeptical view of educational reform. *Journal of Teacher Education, 38*(3), 9–12.

Rorty, R. (1982). *Consequences of pragmatism.* Sussex: Harvester Press.

Rose, N. (1990). *Governing the soul: The shaping of the private self.* New York: Routledge and Kegan Paul.

Ross, E., & Hannay, L. (1986). Towards a critical theory of reflective inquiry. *Journal of Teacher Education, 37*(4), 9–15.

Roth, J. (1974). Professionalism: The sociologist's decoy. *Sociology of Work and Occupations, 1*(1), 6–23.

Salter, B., & Tapper, T. (1981). *Education, politics and the state.* London: Grant McIntyre.

Sarup, M. (1988). *An introductory guide to poststructuralism and postmodernism.* Hemel Hempstead: Harvester Wheatsheaf.

Sawer, M. (Ed.). (1982). *Australia and the new right.* Sydney: George Allen and Unwin.

Schön, D. (1987). *Educating the reflective practitioner.* San Francisco: Jossey Bass.

Schools Council. (1989). *Teacher Quality: An issues paper.* Canberra: Australian Government Printing Service.

Schubert, W. (1989). Reconceptualising and the matter of paradigms. *Journal of Teacher Education, 40*(1), 27–32.

Sellars, N. (1988). The effects of practice teaching on the concerns of pre-service primary teachers. *The South Pacific Journal of Teacher Education, 16*(3), 21–32.

Sewell, W. (1992). A theory of structure: Duality, agency and transformation. *American Journal of Sociology, 98*(1), 1–29.

Shaker, P., & Kridel, C. (1989). The return to experience: A reconceptualist call. *Journal of Teacher Education, 40*(1), 2–8.

Shaker, P., & Ullrich, W. (1987). Reconceptualizing the debate over the general education of teachers. *Journal of Teacher Education, 38*(1), 11–15.

Shulman, L. (1987). Knowledge and teaching: Foundations of the new reform. *Harvard Educational Review, 57*, 1–22.

Simon, P. (1988). For a pedagogy of possibility. *Critical Pedagogy Networker, 1*(1), 1–4.

Simpson, R., & Simpson, L. (1969). Women and bureaucracy in the semi-professions. In A. Etzioni (Ed.), *The semi-professions and their organization* (pp. 196–256). Englewood Cliffs, NJ: Prentice Hall.

Slee, R. (1988). Policy development: Discipline or control? In R. Slee (Ed.), *Discipline and schools: A curriculum perspective* (pp. 2–27). Melbourne: Macmillan.

Smiles, S. (1859/1986). *Self-help.* (George Bull, abridger). London: Sedgwick and Jackson.

Smith, R., & Zantiotis, A. (1988a). Practical teacher education and the avant garde. *Journal of Curriculum Theorizing, 8*(2), 77–106.

Smith, R., & Zantiotis, A. (1988b). The practical: Teacher education's systems virus. *Critical Pedagogy Networker, 1*(4), 1–5.

Smyth, J. (1991). International perspectives on teacher collegiality: A labour process discussion based on the concept of teachers' work. *British Journal of Sociology of Education, 12*(3), 323–346.

Smyth, W. (1987). *A rationale for teachers' critical pedagogy: A handbook.* Geelong: Deakin University Press.

Sockett, H. (1987). Has Shulman got the strategy right? *Harvard Educational Review, 57*(2), 208–220.

Speedy, G. (1990). *Discipline review of teacher education in mathematics and science* (Report Extracts Vol. 1). Victoria: Australian Council of Educational Research.

Sprinthall, N., & Theis-Sprinthall, L. (1983). The need for theoretical frameworks in educating teachers: A cognitive developmental perspective. In K. Howey & W. Gardner (Eds.), *The education of teachers* (pp. 74–97). New York: Longman.

Street, A. (1990). Thinking, acting, reflecting: A critical ethnography of nursing. *Critical Pedagogy Networker, 3*(1), 1–8.

Taylor, P. (1975). A study of the concerns of students in a post graduate certificate in education course. *British Journal of Teacher Education, 1*(2), 151–161.

Terdiman, R. (1985). *Discourse/counter-discourse: The theory and practices of symbolic resistance in nineteenth century France.* Ithaca, NY: Cornell University Press.

Tesch, R. (1989, March). *Planning qualitative research: How much can be done in advance?* Paper presented at the annual meeting of the American Educational Research Association, San Francisco.

Thompson, J. (1984). *Studies in the theory of ideology.* Cambridge: Polity Press.

Tickle, L. (1987). *Learning teaching, teaching teaching.* London: The Falmer Press.

Tisher, R., & Wideen, M. (1990). *Research in teacher education: International perspectives.* London: The Falmer Press.

Tomm, W. (1989). The effects of feminist approaches on research methodologies, as cited in P. Lather (1991a). *Feminist research in education: Within/against.* Geelong: Deakin University Press.

Toomey, R. (1989). Producing quality teachers for tomorrow's Australia. *The South Pacific Journal of Teacher Education, 17*(1), 47–56.

Tripp, D. (1990). The ideology of educational research. *Discourse: The Australian Journal of Educational Studies, 10*(2), 51–74.

Tymitz-Wolf, B. (1984). The new vocationalism and teacher education. *Journal of Teacher Education, 35*(1), 21–25.

Valli, L., & Tom, A. (1988). How adequate are the knowledge base frameworks in teacher education. *Journal of Teacher Education, 39*(5), 5–12.

Walker, R. (1985). *Doing research: A handbook for teachers.* London: Methuen.

Walkerdine, V. (1986). Post-structuralist theory and everyday social practices: The family and the school. In S. Wilkinson (Ed.), *Feminist social psychology: Developing theory and practice* (pp. 57–76). Milton Keynes: The Open University Press.

Wallace, M. (1987). A historical review of action research: Some implications for the education of teachers in their managerial role. *Journal of Education for Teaching, 13*(2), 97–115.

Warner, D., & Swindell, M. (n.d.). *Interviews with beginning secondary teachers: Problems of beginning teaching.* Unpublished manuscript. Brisbane, Australia: Brisbane College of Advanced Education.

Weber, S. (1986, April). *Teacher education: The professor's point of view.* Paper presented at the annual meeting of the American Educational Research Association, San Francisco.

Weedon, C. (1987). *Feminist practice and poststructuralist theory.* Oxford: Basil Blackwell.

Westcott, M. (1979). Feminist criticism of the social sciences. *Harvard Educational Review, 49*(4), 422–430.

Wexler, P. (1987). *Social analysis of education: After the new sociology.* New York: Routledge and Kegan Paul.

Wildman, T., & Niles, J. (1987). Reflective teachers: Tensions between abstractions and realities. *Journal of Teacher Education, 38*(4), 25–31.

Williams, C. (1989, November). *Preservice teachers' perceptions of school climate before and after completion of a secondary field-based practicum.* Paper presented at the annual meeting of the Midsouth Educational Research Association, Little Rock.

Wolff, J. (1985). The invisible flaneuse: Women and the literature of modernity. *Theory, Culture and Society, 2*(3), 37–46.

Wolin, S. (1983). From progress to modernization: The conservative turn. *Democracy, 3*(4), 9–21.

Yates, L. (1990). *Theory/practice dilemmas: Gender, knowledge and education.* Geelong: Deakin University Press.

Yeats, W. (1975). The second coming. In *The Norton anthology of poetry* (revised shorter ed.). New York: W. W. Norton.

Young, M. (Ed.). (1971). *Knowledge and control.* London: Collier Macmillan.

Zeichner, K. (1981–82). Reflective teaching and field-based experience in teacher education. *Interchange, 12*(4), 1–22.

Zeichner, K. (1986). Teacher socialisation and the practice of teaching. *Education and Society, 3*(1), 25–37.

Zeichner, K., & Tabachnick, R. (1981). Are the effects of university education washed out by school experience? *Journal of Teacher Education, 32*(3), 7–10.

Zeichner, K., & Teitelbaum, K. (1982). Personalized and inquiry-oriented teacher education: An analysis of two approaches to the development of curriculum for field based experiences. *Journal of Education for Teaching, 8*(2), 95–117.

INDEX

ABOUT THE AUTHOR

Erica McWilliam is a Senior Lecturer in the School of Cultural and Policy Studies (Faculty of Education) at the Queensland University of Technology in Australia. Her own teaching experience spans 25 years, 19 of which have been spent in high schools and 6 in initial teacher training. Having taught in public and private schools in both rural and urban areas, she maintains links with schools through conducting in-service workshops for both teachers and students. She has published many articles on teacher education policy and critical feminist practice, and is a co-editor of *Unfinished Business: Reshaping the Teacher Education Industry in the 1990's* (1993) published by University of Central Queensland Press.